A. W. Bacheler

Reference Handbook of American History by the Library Method for

Secondary Schools

Period of the Constitution, 1789-1889

A. W. Bacheler

Reference Handbook of American History by the Library Method for Secondary Schools
Period of the Constitution, 1789-1889

ISBN/EAN: 9783337202903

Printed in Europe, USA, Canada, Australia, Japan

Cover: Foto ©ninafisch / pixelio.de

More available books at **www.hansebooks.com**

REFERENCE HANDBOOK

OF

AMERICAN HISTORY

BY THE

LIBRARY METHOD

FOR

SECONDARY SCHOOLS

PERIOD OF THE CONSTITUTION

1789 — 1889

BY

A. W. BACHELER

"The intelligent study of American History is the surest method of inculcating American patriotism." — *Newspaper print.*

BOSTON
LEE AND SHEPARD PUBLISHERS
NO. 10 MILK STREET
1895

"NO SUBJECT CAN BE LEARNED FROM A SINGLE BOOK."
Woodrow Wilson.

TO THE TEACHER OF AMERICAN HISTORY

THE Manual now offered for use in Secondary Schools is the outgrowth of several years' study of the problem of teaching History in a large New England High School. The earlier method, by the use of a single text-book, uniform for the entire class, was beset with difficulties, brought little enthusiasm to the class-room, shut in the pupil's view to the narrow limits of a single author, and left surprisingly little room for the free use of authorities or the interchange of class-room opinions.

Discussion was debarred, for there was nothing to discuss. The opinions of the one author in use being accepted as the opinion of the class, no incentive remained to wider investigation or the assimilation of variant views. The Library Method, now so generally adopted by the best schools, is the outcome of a study of these difficulties, and this Manual is but one of several attempts to render lighter the work of the teacher of American history, and that of the pupil more varied and interesting.

Care has been taken, in making the choice of topics, to select only those whose bearing upon the history of the country has been important and permanent; the trivial and evanescent have been discarded. Chronological arrangement has, in the main, been preserved, but where sequence of cause and effect, or the close relation of subjects somewhat widely separated in point of time, has seemed to demand it, chronology has been disregarded.

To the Teacher of American History

Experience has seemed to emphasize the following suggestions:

Let the pupil be encouraged, or, better, required to consult more than one authority on the topics which constitute a day's lesson. Guard carefully against the tendency of the careless to use but a single authority, and that the briefest and most elementary the library affords.

However desirable that the entire list of books appended to this Manual be accessible, it should not be considered necessary before the adoption of the Library Method. There is always a library within a library, and, while the general field is large, it is possible to make a judicious and limited selection, the cost of which shall be within the means of any town; the interested teacher will not long lack for ways of enlarging the scope of the history library. The kindly interest of a private purse, or the possibilities of a school exhibition, or the school-lecture course, will easily supply what the scantiness of the town appropriation forbids. A minimum list for a class of thirty pupils might include, perhaps, the following:

One copy each of

>Blaine's Twenty Years of Congress.
>Bryant & Gay's History of U.S.
>Draper's Civil War.
>Hildreth's History of U.S.
>Greeley's American Conflict.
>Lalor's Cyclopædia of Politics.
>McMaster's History of the People.
>Stanwood's Presidential Elections.
>Rhodes' History of the U.S.
>Taussig's Tariff History.
>Wilson's Rise and Fall.
>Mrs. Richardson's Story of our Country.
>The four volumes of C. C. Coffin.

To the Teacher of American History

Add to these three copies each of the Epochs of American History Series (the two later volumes of Hart and Wilson).
    Fiske's History of the U.S.
    Higginson's Young Folks' History.
    Johnston's History of U.S.
    Montgomery's History of U.S.
    Schouler's History of the U.S.
    Thomas' History of U.S.

A total of seventy-three volumes; and the class would be tolerably well equipped for good work. Nor should the teacher omit from his list the abundant material which might be classed under "*original sources*," such as the Lowell and Old South Series of our great State papers. The Declaration, Articles of Confederation, Constitution, the Ordinance of 1787, the Inaugurals, and Farewell Address of Washington, and many others, all of which are now so cheaply and readily accessible as to remove all objection on the score of expense.

The value of memorizing the topics under the groupings of the Manual seems to be proved. Two such groupings are made in the present work, one by Presidential Administrations, the other, and the larger, by Historical Periods.

For example, the second, or period of "Federalist Supremacy," includes the two administrations of Washington and the one of John Adams. To memorize the topics under such a group is deemed an important feature of the Library Method.

The outline map in the hands of each pupil should steadily accompany the progress of the class, growing with its growth. When new territory is added to the original area, or a new State admitted to the Union, or an important event occurs, let the map indicate this with date, and initials of the President under whom the event occurred. The series of outline maps issued by D. C. Heath & Co. of Boston are admirably adapted for this purpose.

Lastly, there is abundant room for the play of the occasional class discussion, or the more formal essay upon topics in which special interest has been evinced as the study has progressed. The interest and alertness of the teacher will not fail to improve upon, and enlarge these few suggestions out of a past experience.

A. W. B.

JULY 4, 1894.

LIST OF THE BOOKS REFERRED TO IN THIS VOLUME

Abbott John S. C. . . . The History of the Civil War in America . . . . 2 v. *H. B.*
Abbott Willis J. . . . Battlefields of '61 . . . . *D., M. & Co.*
Adams Henry . . . . . History of the United States of America during the Administrations of Jefferson and Madison . . . . 6 v. *Scr. Sons.*
Anderson John J. . . . New Grammar School History of the United States . . . . *M., M. & Co.*
Bancroft George . . History of the United States of America, Author's Last Edition . . . . . 6 v. *App. & Co.*
Bancroft Hubert H. . The Northwest Coast . . . . *Bancroft Co.*
Battles and Leaders . . . . 4 v. *C. Pub. Co.*
Benton Thomas H. . . Thirty Years' View, from 1820-1850 . . 2 v. *App. & Co.*
Blaine James G. . . . Twenty Years of Congress, from Lincoln to Garfield . . . . 2 v. *H. B.*
Bryant & Gay . . . . . A Popular History of the United States, 4 v. *Scr. Sons.*
Bryce James . . . . The American Commonwealth . . . . 2 v. *Mac. & Co.*
Campaigns of the Civil War . . . . . 13 v. *Scr. Sons.*
Coffin Chas. Carleton . Building the Nation . . . . *H. & Bros.*
 "   "   "   . Drumbeat of the Nation . . . . *H. & Bros.*
 "   "   "   Marching to Victory . . . . *H. & Bros.*
 "   "   "   . Redeeming the Republic . . . . *H. & Bros.*
Comte de Paris . . . . History of the Civil War in America . 4 v. *P. & C.*
Cooper J. Fennimore . History of the Navy of the United States . . . .
Curtis George Ticknor, Constitutional History of the United States . . . . 2 v. *H. & Bros.*
De Trobriand Regis . Four Years with the Army of the Potomac . . . .
Draper John W. . . . History of the American Civil War . . 3 v. *H. & Bros.*
Eggleston Edward . . A History of the United States . . . . *App. & Co.*
Fiske John . . . . . . The Critical Period of American History . . . . *H., M. & Co.*

(vii)

List of the Books referred to in this Volume

Fiske John	A History of the United States	*H., M. & Co.*
Frothingham	The Rise of the Republic	*L., B. & Co.*
Greeley Horace	The American Conflict	*2 v. Case & Co.*
Grimke A. H.	Life of Charles Sumner	*Funk & W.*
Hart A. B.	Formation of the American Union	*3 v. L., G. & Co.*
Haswell John H.	Treaties and Conventions	*G. P. O.*
Higginson Thomas W.	Young Folks' History of the United States	*L., G. & Co.*
Hildreth Richard	History of the United States of America	*6 v. H. & Bros.*
Irving-Fiske	Washington and his Country	*Ginn & Co.*
Jay Wm.	A Review of the History of the Mexican War	
Johnston Alexander	History of American Politics	*H. H. & Co.*
" "	A History of the United States	*H. H. & Co.*
Lalor John J.	Cyclopædia of Political Science	*3 v. Mer. & Co.*
Lossing Benson J.	Field Book of the War of 1812	*G. S. Lester.*
" " "	Field Book of the Civil War	*G. S. Lester.*
Lovell A.	American History Leaflets	*13 Nos. L. & Co.*
Maclay Edgar S.	A History of the United States Navy	*2 v. App. & Co.*
McMaster John Bach	A History of the People of the United States	*5 v. App. & Co.*
Montgomery D. H.	The Leading Facts of American History	*Ginn & Co.*
Moore Frank	The Rebellion Record	*12 v. D. Van N.*
Morse John T., Jr.	[*Editor*] American Statesmen Series	*12 v. H., M. & Co.*
Nicolay & Hay	Abraham Lincoln, A History	*10 v. C. Pub. Co.*
	Old South Leaflets	*13 Nos. H. & Co.*
Parton James	Life of Aaron Burr	*Mason Bros.*
" "	Life of Andrew Jackson	*Mason Bros.*
Patton Jacob H.	Four Hundred Years of American History	*2 v. F., H. & H.*
Pollard Edward A.	The Lost Cause	*Treat & Co.*
Porter David D.	The Naval History of the Civil War	*S. Pub. Co.*
Rhodes James Ford	History of the United States from the Compromise of 1850	*2 v. H. & Bros.*
Richardson Abbie S.	The History of Our Country	*H., M. & Co.*
Roosevelt Theodore	The Naval War of 1812	*Put. Sons.*
Sargent Nathan	Public Men and Events	*2 v. Lip. & Co.*
Schouler James	History of the United States of America	*6 v. D., M. & Co.*
Scudder Horace E.	[*Editor*] American Commonwealth Series	*12 v. H., M. & Co.*
Sheldon-Barnes	Studies in American History	*H. & Co.*
Smith Goldwin	The United States	*Mac. & Co.*

List of the Books referred to in this Volume ix

Stanwood Edward A. . . History of Presidential Elections . . . *H., M. & Co.*
Stevens Alexander H., A Constitutional View of the War between the States . . . . *2 v. N. Pub. Co.*
Stevens C. Ellis . . . Sources of the Constitution . . . . . .
Taussig . . . . Tariff History of the United States . . *Put. Sons.*
Thomas Allen C. . . . . A History of the United States . . . . *H. & Co.*
Von Holst Hermann . The Constitutional and Political History of the United States . . . . . *6 v. C. & Co.*
Walker Francis A. . . History of the Second Army Corps . . *Scr. Sons.*
Williams Alfred M. . . Life of Sam Houston . . . . *H., M. & Co.*
Wilson Henry . . . . History of the Rise and Fall of the Slave Power in America . . . . . *3 v. H., M. & Co.*
Wilson Woodrow . . . Division and Reunion . . . . *L., G. & Co.*
Winsor Justin . . . . Narrative and Critical History of America . . . . *8 v. H., M. & Co.*

186 volumes. 67 works.

In the abbreviations, App. & Co. stands for D. Appleton & Co.; H. B. for Henry Bill; Case & Co. for O. D. Case & Co.; C. & Co. for Callahan & Co.; C. Pub. Co. for Century Publishing Co.; D., M. & Co. for Dodd, Mead & Co.; F., H. & H. for Fords, Howard & Hulbert; Funk & W. for Funk & Wagnalls; G. P. O. for Government Printing Office; H. & Bros. for Harper & Brothers; H. & Co. for D. C. Heath & Co.; H. H. & Co. for Henry Holt & Co.; H., M. & Co. for Houghton, Mifflin & Co.; L., B. & Co. for Little, Brown & Co.; Lip. & Co. for J. B. Lippincott & Co.; L., G. & Co. for Longmans, Green & Co.; L. & Co. for A. Lovell & Co.; Mac. & Co. for Macmillan & Co.; M., M. & Co. for Maynard, Merrill & Co.; Mer. & Co. for Chas. E. Merrill & Co.; N. Pub. Co. for National Publishing Co.; P. & C. for Porter & Coates; Put. Sons for G. P. Putnam's Sons; Scr. Sons for Charles Scribner's Sons; S. Pub. Co. for The Sherman Publishing Co.; Treat & Co. for E. B. Treat & Co.; D. Van N. for D. Van Nostrand.

HANDBOOK OF AMERICAN HISTORY

THE CONFEDERATION

The Critical Period 1781-1789

The Articles of Confederation

First attempt at organized, national Government, Mar. 1, 1781. See No. 2, Old South Leaflets, D. C. Heath & Co.

- Bancroft, vi. 12-19.
- Coffin, Building the Nation, 17.
- Curtis, Constitutional Hist., i. 86.
- Eggleston, 198.
- Fiske, Critical Period, 93-96.
- Frothingham, Rise of the Republic, 576-579.
- Hart, Epochs Am. Hist., 93-95.
- Hildreth, iii. 398, 399.
- Johnston, 136-139.
- Lalor, Cyclopædia, i. 574-577.
- Patton, Four Hundred Years of Am. History, ii. 1161.
- Schouler, i. 14-16.
- Thomas, 133.
- Von Holst, i. 20.
- Winsor, vii. 215-232.

Defects of the Confederation

"Perpetual" proved to be eight years. See Art. 13.
"To be more exposed in the eyes of the world, and more contemptible than we already are, is hardly possible."
Washington.

- Bancroft, vi. 19-23, 212.
- Bryant & Gay, iv. 99.
- Coffin, Building the Nation, 17.
- Curtis, Constitutional Hist., i. 101, 102, 104, 320-323, 334, 351, 361, 556.
- Eggleston, 198.
- Fiske, Critical Period, 97-105.
- Fiske, Hist. of U.S., 247.
- Frothingham, Rise of the Republic, 578.
- Hart, Epochs Am. History, 109, 117-119.
- Higginson, 214, 215.

Defects of the Confederation
(Continued)

- Hildreth, iii. 402-404.
- Irving-Fiske, 492.
- Johnston, 139.
- Johnston, Hist. Am. Politics, 7-8.
- Lalor, Cyclopædia, i. 548, 575, 576.
- McMaster, i. 131, 132.
- Montgomery, 186.
- Schouler, i. 16, 22, 23.
- Sheldon-Barnes, 196-199.
- Smith, Goldwin, 119-121.
- Thomas, 134.
- Von Holst, i, 40-45.

The Newburgh Addresses

- Bancroft, vi. 59-62, 71-74.
- Bryant & Gay, iv. 86-88.
- Curtis, Constitutional Hist., i. 106-112.
- Fiske, Critical Period, 108-110.
- Hart, Epochs Am. History, 106.
- Hildreth, iii. 430-433.
- Lalor, Cyclopædia, i. 576.
- Lodge, Life of Hamilton, 40-43.
- Lodge, Life of Washington, i. 327.
- McMaster, i. 181-183.
- Patton, Four Hundred Years of Am. History, i. 557.
- Thomas, 131.
- Von Holst, i. 40.

Disorders in the States

Shays' Rebellion.

- Bancroft, vi. 200.
- Bryant & Gay, iv. 96-99.
- Coffin, Building the Nation, 16, 17.
- Curtis, Constitutional Hist., i. 179-182.
- Fiske, Critical Period, 177-183.
- Fiske, Hist. of U.S., 298.
- Frothingham, Rise of the Republic, 588.
- Gay, Life of Madison, 76-87.
- Hale, Story of Mass., 300-303.
- Hart, Epochs Am. History, 111-113.
- Higginson, 214.
- Hildreth, iii. 474-477.

The Critical Period

Disorders in the States
(*Continued*)

- Irving-Fiske, 492-495.
- Johnston, 139.
- Lalor, Cyclopædia, i. 577.
- Lodge, Life of Washington, ii. 17-27.
- McMaster, i. 306-330.
- Montgomery, 185, 186.
- Morse, Life of Jefferson, 90, 91.
- Patton, i. 562.
- Schouler, i. 32-34.
- Smith, Goldwin, 121.
- Thomas, 134.
- Von Holst, i. 44-46.

Ordinance of 1787 For the Government of the Northwest Territory.

Almost the final act of the Congress of the Confederation, "A document inferior only to the Federal Constitution." "One of the three title deeds of American constitutional Liberty."
George F. Hoar.

See No. 13 Old South Leaflets, for full text of the Ordinance.

- Bancroft, vi. 116-119.
- Bryant & Gay, iv. 109, 110.
- Curtis, Constitutional Hist., i. 535-537.
- Eggleston, 232.
- Fiske, Critical Period, 203-207.
- Hart, Epochs Am. History, 108.
- Higginson, 231, 254.
- Hildreth, iii. 527-529.
- Johnston, 146.
- Lalor, Cyclopædia, iii. 30-33.
- McMaster, i. 150, 155, 156; ii. 478.
- Montgomery, 187.
- Morse, Life of Jefferson, 75.
- Patton, i. 566-567.
- Rhodes, Hist. of U.S., i. 16.
- Schouler, i. 100, 101.
- Sheldon-Barnes, 199-202.
- Thomas, 146, 147.
- Wilson, Epochs Am. Hist., 131.
- Winsor, vii. 537-543.

The Constitutional Convention of 55 Delegates May 14-Sept. 17, 1787

- Bancroft, vi. 210, 211.
- Bryce, Am. Commonwealth, i. 639.
- Bryant & Gay, iv. 100-102.
- Coffin, Building the Nation, 17, 18.
- Curtis, Constitutional Hist., 253, 257, 261, 263, 265, 273, 277, 282, 290, 295.

4   Handbook of American History

The Constitutional Convention of 55 Delegates May 14– Sept. 17, 1787
(Continued)

- Eggleston, 198.
- Fiske, Critical Period, 222-229.
- Fiske, Hist. of U.S., 248.
- Frothingham, Rise of the Republic, 589, 590.
- Gay, Life of Madison, 88-97.
- Hart, Epochs Am. History, 121-123.
- Higginson, 215.
- Hildreth, iii. 482-526.
- Irving-Fiske, 496-498.
- Johnston, Hist. Am. Politics, 10, 11.
- Johnston, 140, 141.
- Lalor, Cyclopædia, i. 637-640.
- Lodge, Life of Washington, ii. 29-37.
- Lodge, Life of Hamilton, 57-59.
- McMaster, i. 416-423.
- Montgomery, 188-189.
- Patton, i. 564-566.
- Richardson, Story of our Country, 284.
- Schouler, i. 36-47.
- Sheldon-Barnes, 203-206.
- Thomas, 135, 136.
- Von Holst, i. 52-55.
- Winsor, vii. 237-251.

Sources of the Constitution

Lovell's Am. Hist. Leaflets, No. 8, Text of the Constitution.

- Bancroft, vi. 441-451.
- Bryce, Am. Commonwealth, i. 25-28, 640-643.
- Coffin, Building the Nation, 21.
- Curtis, Constitutional Hist., i. 452, 514, 515.
- Fiske, Critical Period, 289-300.
- Gay, Life of Madison, 90-97.
- Hart, Epochs Am. History, 6, 7, 124, 125.
- Hildreth, iii. 482.
- McMaster, i. 438, 439.
- Schouler, i. 38.
- Stevens, C. Ellis, Sources of the Constitution.
- Von Holst, i. 61-63.
- Winsor, vii. 237, 238.

The Critical Period 5

The Three Great Compromises

1. Equality of States in the Senate.
2. Three-fifths of the slaves reckoned in apportionment.
3. Forbidding prohibition of slave-trade till 1808.

Bancroft, vi. 228, 255, 266, 316-320.
Bryant & Gay, iv. 102.
Coffin, Building the Nation, 19-21.
Curtis, Const. Hist., 386, 387, 405, 406, 416-418.
Fiske, Critical Period, 256-267.
Gay, Life of Madison, 98-114.
Greeley, Am. Conflict, i. 43-49.
Hart, Epochs Am. History, 125-127.
Hildreth, iii. 486, 489, 496, 518.
Lalor, Cyclopædia, i. 547, 549.
McMaster, i. 442, 443, 446, 449, 450.
Montgomery, 188, 189.
Patton, i. 565, 566.
Schouler, i. 41, 42.
Sheldon-Barnes, 204-206.
Thomas, 136, 137.
Winsor, vii. 239.

The Ratification by States

The Federalist. The first number written by Hamilton in the cabin of a sloop, on the Hudson. See No. 12, Old South Leaflets, Federalist.

Bancroft, vi. 389, 390, 392, 395, 406, 413, 420, 437, 438, 452, 453.
Bryant & Gay, iv. 103, 104.
Bryce, Am. Commonwealth, i. 22-24.
Coffin, Building the Nation, 22.
Curtis, Const. Hist., i. 641, 645, 646, 647, 649, 656, 660, 661, 683, 687, 692.
Fiske, Critical Period, 314-340, 341-343.
Frothingham, Rise of the Republic, 599, 603.
Gay, Life of Madison, 115-127.
Higginson, 215.
Hildreth, iii. 535-539.
Johnston, 143.
Johnston, Hist. Am. Politics, 15, 16.
Lalor, Cyclopædia, i. 637-640.
Lodge, Life of Hamilton, 66-70.
McMaster, i. 473, 476-479, 485, 487, 491, 499.
Patton, i. 566.
Richardson, Story of our Country, 285, 286.

The Ratification by States *(Continued)*		Schouler, i. 58-66. Thomas, 137-140. Winsor, vii. 257-260.

Summary of the Critical Period

1781–1789	The Confederation. Defects in the Articles.
1783	The Newburgh Addresses. Peace with Great Britain.
1784	Cession of Territory by Virginia.
1786	The Convention at Annapolis. Shays' Rebellion.
1787	The Constitutional Convention. The Ordinance of 1787.
1788	The Ratification by States.
1789	Establishment of the New Government.

The Period of Federalist Supremacy 1789–1801

First Administration of George Washington 1789-1793

Establishment of the New Government and First Inauguration of Washington
- Bryant & Gay, iv. 104, 105.
- Century Mag., Vol. 37, No. 6.
- Coffin, Building the Nation, 24-26.
- Eggleston, 203.
- Fiske, Critical Period, 348-350.
- Frothingham, Rise of the Republic, 603.
- Hart, Epochs Am. Hist., 143.
- Higginson, 216-219.
- Hildreth, iv. 54-62.
- Irving-Fiske, 500-506.
- Johnston, 143, 148.
- Lodge, Life of Washington, ii. 43-50.
- McMaster, i. 530-532, 538-540.
- Morse, Life of Jefferson, 96.
- Montgomery, 192.
- Richardson, Story of our Country, 286, 287.
- Schouler, i. 74-80, 82-93, 107-109.
- Sheldon-Barnes, 211, 212.
- Stanwood, Pres. Elections, 14-16.
- Thomas, 144-146.
- Von Holst, i. 80-84.

The First Cabinet
- Bryce, Am. Commonwealth, i. 81.
- Bryant & Gay, iv. 105, 122.
- Hart, Epochs of Am. History, 144.
- Hildreth, iv. 108, 131.
- Johnston, 150.
- Lodge, Life of Hamilton, 84, 85.
- Lodge, Life of Washington, ii. 63-69.
- McMaster, i. 566.
- Montgomery, 192, 193.
- Morse, Life of Jefferson, 96, 97.

The First Cabinet
(Continued)
- Patton, i. 574, 575.
- Schouler, i. 109, 110.
- Sheldon-Barnes, 213.
- Smith, Goldwin, 130, 138.
- Thomas, 147.

Division of Parties Federalist and Anti-Federalist
- Bryant & Gay, iv. 106, 107.
- Bryce, Am. Commonwealth, ii. 5, 6, 16, 23.
- Coffin, Building the Nation, 34, 35.
- Eggleston, 213, 214.
- Fiske, Critical Period, 308-310.
- Fiske, Hist. of U.S., 261, 262.
- Frothingham, Rise of the Republic, 598, 599.
- Gay, Life of Madison, 172-192.
- Hart, Epochs Am. History, 155, 156.
- Higginson, 221.
- Hildreth, iv. 25-40.
- Irving-Fiske, 511, 512.
- Lalor, Cyclopædia, i. 769-771; ii. 165-172.
- Lodge, Life of Hamilton, 136-142.
- Lodge, Life of Washington, ii. 61, 232.
- McMaster, i. 567.
- Montgomery, 191, 192.
- Morse, Life of Jefferson, 144, 145.
- Patton, i. 581.
- Richardson, Story of our Country, 286.
- Sargent, Public Men and Events, i. 17, 18.
- Schouler, i. 53-56.
- Sheldon-Barnes, 209.
- Smith, Goldwin, 150.
- Thomas, 151.
- Von Holst, i. 77, 78.
- Winsor, vii. 267, 268.
- Young, Friends and Foes of Const., 73.

First Admission of New States
Vermont 1791
Kentucky 1792
Tennessee 1796
- Bryant & Gay, iv. 83.
- Eggleston, 257, 258.
- Hart, Epochs Am. History, 152.
- Higginson, 229, 230.
- Irving-Fiske, 538.

The Period of Federalist Supremacy

First Admission of New States
(Continued)

- Johnston, 37, 151, 152.
- Hildreth, iv. 267, 268.
- Lalor, Cyclopædia, iii. 994.
- McMaster, ii. 35.
- Richardson, Story of our Country, 291.
- Schouler, i. 149, 150, 314.
- Sheldon-Barnes, 282.
- Thomas, 149.
- Winsor, vii. 268, 280, 530.

Hamilton's Great Measures in Finance

1. Assumption of State Debts.
2. The First Excise.
3. The Funding of Nat. Debt.
4. Incorporation of a Bank.

"It is certain that no other measures of the Federal Government contributed, in even an approximate degree, to the actual consolidation of the Union."
Von Holst.

- Bryant & Gay, iv. 105, 106.
- Bryce, Am. Commonwealth, i. 81.
- Coffin, Building the Nation, 34.
- Eggleston, 215.
- Fiske, Hist. of U.S., 260, 261.
- Hart, Epochs Am. History, 146-151.
- Hildreth, iv. 213-215, 253, 254, 262-265.
- Johnston, Hist. Am. Politics, 21-23.
- Lodge, Life of Hamilton, 92-104, 126-129, 131.
- Lodge, Life of Washington, ii. 104-122.
- McMaster, i. 568-578, 582; ii. 28-32.
- Montgomery, 193, 194.
- Morse, Life of Jefferson, 97-102.
- Patton, i. 575-577, 581, 582.
- Schouler, i. 130-142, 158-162.
- Sheldon-Barnes, 213.
- Thomas, 148, 149.
- Von Holst, i. 94, 95.
- Winsor, vii. 268.

Second Administration of George Washington 1793-1797

The Whiskey Insurrection

- Bryant & Gay, iv. 118, 119.
- Coffin, Building the Nation, 34.
- Eggleston, 217, 218.
- Fiske, Hist. of U.S., 263..
- Hart, Epochs Am. History, 163, 164.
- Hildreth, iv. 373-376.
- Irving-Fiske, 510, 511.

10   *Handbook of American History*

**The Whiskey
Insurrection**
(Continued)
> Johnston, Hist. Am. Politics, 34.
> Johnston, 150.
> Lalor, Cyclopædia, iii. 1108-1111.
> Lodge, Life of Hamilton, 180-185.
> Lodge, Life of Washington, ii. 120-128.
> McMaster, ii. 41-43.
> Montgomery, 197, 198.
> Patton, i. 585, 586.
> Richardson, 294.
> Schouler, i. 214, 275-280.
> Stevens, Life of Gallatin, 69-99.
> Thomas, 149, 150.
> Von Holst, i. 94-102.

**Eli Whitney and
the Cotton Gin**

The second of our great industrial inventions, Hargreaves and Arkwright's Spinning Jenny, 1767, being the first.
> Bryant & Gay, iv. 261.
> Coffin, Building the Nation, 73-77.
> Eggleston, 374.
> Fiske, Hist. of U.S., 302.
> Greeley, Am. Conflict, i. 57-66.
> Higginson, 225, 226.
> Irving-Fiske, 537, 538.
> Johnston, Hist. Am. Politics, 86.
> Johnston, 159, 160.
> Lalor, Cyclopædia, iii. 729.
> McMaster, ii. 161-163.
> Montgomery, 195-197.
> Patton, ii. 700.
> Rhodes, i. 25.
> Sheldon-Barnes, 282.
> Thomas, 150.

Citizen Genet
> Bryant & Gay, iv. 123.
> Coffin, Building the Nation, 59-61.
> Fiske, Hist. of U.S., 264, 265.
> Hart, Epochs Am. History, 159, 160.
> Hildreth, iv. 412-440.
> Irving-Fiske, 512.
> Johnston, Hist. Am. Politics, 29-31.
> Johnston, 154.
> Lalor, Cyclopædia, ii. 327-331.

The Period of Federalist Supremacy

Citizen Genet
(*Continued*)

- Lossing, Field Book, 78-82.
- McMaster, ii. 98-105, 137-142.
- Montgomery, 194.
- Morse, Life of Jefferson, 149, 152-162.
- Patton, i. 583, 584.
- Richardson, 293.
- Schouler, i. 246-256.
- Smith, Goldwin, 144, 145.
- Thomas, 152.
- Von Holst, i. 112-118.
- Winsor, vii. 464.

Influence of the French Revolution on American Politics

"It was a case of *Liberty*, versus Order."
Bryce.

- Bryant & Gay, iv. 122, 123.
- Bryce, Am. Commonwealth, ii. 6.
- Hart, Epochs Am. History, 157.
- Higginson, 220, 221.
- Hildreth, iv. 411-415.
- Irving-Fiske, 512.
- Johnston, Hist. Am. Politics, 28, 29.
- Johnston, 154.
- Lodge, Life of Washington, 140-143.
- McMaster, ii. 96-98.
- Montgomery, 194.
- Morse, Life of Jefferson, 146-148.
- Patton, i. 582.
- Richardson, 293.
- Schouler, i. 168, 241-243.
- Thomas, 151, 152.
- Von Holst, i. 107, 108.

Jay's Treaty

"When the spotless ermine of the judicial robe fell on John Jay, it touched nothing less spotless than itself."
Daniel Webster

- Bryant & Gay, iv. 123-126.
- Eggleston, 220.
- Fiske, Hist. of U.S., 265.
- Hart, Epochs Am. History, 160-163.
- Haswell, "Treaties and Conventions," 379-394.
- Higginson, 220.
- Hildreth, iv. 539-553.
- Irving-Fiske, 513.
- Johnston, Hist. Am. Politics, 33, 35, 37.

Jay's Treaty
(Continued)

For full text of the treaty, see Haswell, "Treaties and Conventions," 379-394.

- Johnston, 155.
- Lalor, Cyclopædia, ii. 634-638.
- Lodge, Life of Washington, 176-201.
- Lossing, Field Book, 86, 87.
- McMaster, ii. 212-220, 263, 281.
- Montgomery, 198.
- Morse, Life of Jefferson, 169-171.
- Patton, i. 587, 588.
- Schouler, i. 289-296, 308-317.
- Sheldon-Barnes, 282.
- Smith, Goldwin, 146, 147.
- Thomas, 152, 153.
- Von Holst, i. 122-128.
- Winsor, vii. 466-471.

The Farewell Address of Washington

Except Jackson, Washington the only president to issue such an address.

See Old South Leaflets, No. 4, "The Farewell Address."

- Bryce, Am. Commonwealth, i. 52.
- Hildreth, iv. 685, 686.
- Johnston, Hist. Am. Politics, 38.
- Johnston, 156.
- Lalor, Cyclopædia, ii. 160.
- Lodge, Life of Washington, 244-246.
- McMaster, ii. 289, 290.
- Patton, i. 590.
- Schouler, i. 331, 332.
- Sheldon-Barnes, 214.
- Smith, Goldwin, 147.
- Thomas, 153, 154.

Sidelight Studies on Washington's Time

- Daniel Boone, Famous Boy Series.
- Dickens, Tale of Two Cities.
- George Washington, Famous Boy Series.
- Henty, The Reign of Terror.
- Martineau, The Peasant and the Prince.
- Musick, Braddock, A Story of the French and Indian Wars.

Election and Inauguration of John Adams

- Bryant & Gay, iv. 127, 128.
- Bryce, Am. Commonwealth, i. 39.
- Coffin, Building the Nation, 112.
- Eggleston, 221.

The Period of Federalist Supremacy

Election and Inauguration of John Adams
(*Continued*)

"Always an honest man, often a wise one, but sometimes wholly out of his senses."
Ben. Franklin

- Fiske, Hist. of U.S., 266.
- Harper's Mag., Vol. 68, 548-552.
- Hart, Epochs Am. History, 164, 165.
- Higginson, 231, 232.
- Hildreth, iv. 687, 688, 701.
- Irving-Fiske, 513.
- Johnston, Hist. Am. Politics, 39, 40.
- Johnston, 161.
- McMaster, ii. 291, 307.
- Montgomery, 199.
- Morse, Life of Adams, 257-270.
- Morse, Life of Jefferson, 173, 174.
- Richardson, 294, 295.
- Schouler, i. 341-344.
- Stanwood, Presidential Elections, 24-29.
- Thomas, 154, 155.
- Von Holst, i. 132, 133, 138, 139.

Administration of John Adams 1797-1801

Troubles with France

"Millions for defence, but not a cent for tribute."
Pinckney.

Francis Hopkinson's "Hail Columbia."

- Bryant & Gay, iv. 132-134.
- Coffin, Building the Nation, 112-117.
- Eggleston, 221, 222.
- Fiske, Hist. of U.S., 266, 267.
- Hart, Epochs Am. History, 166-168.
- Higginson, 232, 233.
- Hildreth, v. 219-224, 250-253.
- Irving-Fiske, 513-515.
- Johnston, Hist. Am. Politics, 42-44.
- Johnston, 161, 162.
- Lalor, iii. 1122.
- Lossing, Field Book, 93.
- McMaster, ii. 308-313. In parts to 416.
- Morse, Life of John Adams, 273-287.
- Morse, Life of Jefferson, 146-165.
- Montgomery, 199, 200.
- Patton, i. 591-596.
- Richardson, 295.
- Schouler, i. 344-347, 373-392.
- Stevens, Life of Gallatin, 162-166.

Troubles with France
(Continued)

- Smith, Goldwin, 151.
- Thomas, 155, 156.
- Von Holst, i. 131, 139-142.

Alien and Sedition Acts

See Article I. of the Amendments to the Constitution.

- Bryant & Gay, iv. 129, 130.
- Eggleston, 224, 226.
- Fiske, Hist. of U.S., 268, 270.
- Hart, Epochs Am. History, 168-170.
- Higginson, 233.
- Hildreth, v. 215-216, 225-229.
- Irving-Fiske, 515.
- Johnston, Hist. Am. Politics, 44.
- Johnston, 162, 164.
- Lalor, Cyclopædia, i. 56, 58, 771, 772.
- Lossing, 106, 107.
- McMaster, ii. 389, 390, 393, 395, 396.
- Montgomery, 200, 201.
- Morse, Life of John Adams, 287, 288.
- Patton, i. 594; ii. 710.
- Schouler, i. 393-403.
- Smith, Goldwin, 153.
- Thomas, 156, 157.
- Von Holst, i. 141-143.

Virginia and Kentucky Resolutions of 1798

See No. 14 Lovell's Am. History Leaflets.

"That Jefferson was not only an advocate, but the father, of the doctrine of nullification is thus well established."
Von Holst.

- Adams, i. 139-143.
- Bryant & Gay, iv. 130.
- Fiske, Hist. of U.S., 269.
- Gay, Life of Madison, 246-250.
- Greeley, Am. Conflict, i. 83, 84.
- Hart, Epochs Am. History, 170, 171.
- Hildreth, v. 272-277.
- Irving-Fiske, 515, 516.
- Johnston, Hist. Am. Politics, 45-47.
- Lalor, ii. 672-676.
- McMaster, ii. 419-423.
- Montgomery, 200.
- Morse, Life of Jefferson, 193, 194.
- Patton, ii. 711, 712.
- Schouler, i. 423-425.
- Smith, Goldwin, 153.

The Period of Federalist Supremacy

Virginia etc.
(Continued)

{ Thomas, 157.
Von Holst, i. 144-151. }

Death of Washington Dec. 14, 1799

"First in war, first in peace, first in the hearts of his countrymen."
Richard Henry Lee.

"The greatest of good men and the best of great men."
Edward Everett.

{ Bryant & Gay, iv. 135.
Coffin, Building the Nation, 118.
Eggleston, 218.
Hart, Epochs Am. History, 174.
Higginson, 233.
Hildreth, v. 337-340.
Irving-Fiske, 517-522.
Johnston, 165.
Lodge, Life of Washington, ii. 293-298.
Lossing, Field Book, 109-111.
McMaster, ii. 452-454.
Montgomery, 201.
Patton, i. 596, 597.
Richardson, 296.
Schouler, i. 451, 452.
Thomas, 158. }

Vaccination introduced into the United States in 1800 by Benj. Waterhouse of Boston.

Establishment of the Capitol at Washington Nov. 1800

"This is the first case of 'log-rolling' in the history of Congress."
Goldwin Smith.

{ Bryant & Gay, iv. 135.
Eggleston, 222, 223.
Fiske, Hist. of U.S., 262.
Hart, Epochs Am. Hist., 149.
Higginson, 232.
Hildreth, v. 391-395.
Irving-Fiske, 510.
Johnston, Hist. Am. Politics, 49.
Johnston, 164.
Lalor. Cyclopædia, i. 351, 352.
McMaster, ii. 486-489.
Montgomery, 202.
Patton, 598.
Richardson, 296.
Schouler, i. 475, 476.
Smith, Goldwin, 149.
Thomas, 158. }

16   Handbook of American History

Downfall of the Federalist Party and Election of Jefferson

First Election by the House of Representatives

See Constitution Art. II. Sect. 1.

The greatest work of the Party: "That of framing and establishing the more perfect Union."

Bryant & Gay, iv. 143, 144.
Bryce, Am. Commonwealth, ii. 7, 10, 11.
Eggleston, 224, 226.
Fiske, Hist. of U.S., 270.
Hart, Epochs Am. History, 171-175.
Higginson, 233.
Hildreth, v. 414-418.
Irving-Fiske, 522, 523.
Johnston, Hist. Am. Politics, 49.
Johnston, 164.
Lalor, Cyclopædia, ii. 169.
Lodge, Life of Hamilton, 235, 236.
Lossing, Field Book, 108.
McMaster, ii. 417, 419, 509, 510.
Montgomery, 201.
Morse, Life of John Adams, 305-310, 315-329.
Morse, Life of Jefferson, 195-200.
Patton, i. 598.
Schouler, i. 480-482, 487, 488.
Stanwood, Presidential Elections, 30-44.
Thomas, 158, 159.
Von Holst, i. 168-173.

Summary of the Period of Federalist Supremacy 1789-1801

1789
- First Inauguration of Washington.
- The First Cabinet.
- Ratification by North Carolina.

1790
- Ratification by Rhode Island.
- Division of Parties.

1791
- Establishment of a National Bank.
- The Funding of the National Debt.
- Vermont Admitted.

1792   Kentucky Admitted.

1793
- The Cotton-gin Invented.
- Citizen Genet comes from France.
- French Revolution Influences Am. Politics.

1794	Whiskey Insurrection. Wayne's Defeat of the Ohio Indians
1795	Jay's Treaty.
1796	Tennessee Admitted. Election and Inauguration of John Adams. Washington's Farewell Address.
1798	Troubles with France. Alien and Sedition Acts. Virginia and Kentucky Resolutions.
1799	Death of Washington.
1800	Establishment of the Capitol at Washington. Downfall of the Federalist Party. Election of Jefferson.

Period of Republican Supremacy 1801–1809

First Administration of Thomas Jefferson 1801-1805

Inauguration and First Administration of Thomas Jefferson

- Adams, Hist. of U.S., i. 185-217.
- Bryant & Gay, iv. 144. 145, 164-168.
- Eggleston, 226-227.
- Hart, Epochs Am. History, 176-179.
- Higginson, 235.
- Hildreth, v. 419-423.
- Irving-Fiske, 523.
- Johnston, Hist. Am. Politics, 52-54.
- Johnston, 166, 167.
- Lalor, Cyclopædia, ii. 638, 639.
- Lossing, Field Book, 112, 114, 115.
- McMaster, ii. 533-537.
- Montgomery, 201, 202.
- Morse, Life of Jefferson, 200-208.
- Richardson, 297, 298.
- Schouler, ii. 1-4.
- Thomas, 160, 161.
- Von Holst, i. 168, 178.

Barbary Wars and Decatur's Exploit

"The first American vessel of war (the 'George Washington') to visit the Bosphorus entered the Golden Horn with a pirate flag at the mast-head."

- Adams, i. 244-246; ii. 137-140, 425-437.
- Bryant & Gay, iv. 154-161.
- Coffin, Building the Nation, 119-130.
- Eggleston, 228, 229.
- Fiske, Hist. of U.S., 275, 276.
- Hart, Epochs Am. History, 184, 185.
- Higginson, 237, 238.
- Hildreth, v. 482-484, 507-509.
- Irving-Fiske, 525.
- Johnston, 170, 171.
- Lalor, Cyclopædia, i. 55, 56.
- Lossing, Field Book, 116-125.
- Maclay, Hist. of U.S. Navy, i. 214-269.

Period of Republican Supremacy

Barbary Wars and Decatur's Exploit
(Continued)
- McMaster, ii. 588, 593, 602.
- Montgomery, 203.
- Patton, i. 601-603.
- Richardson, 301-306.
- Schouler, ii. 16-18, 67, 68, 92-94.
- Thomas, 163, 164.
- Winsor, vii. 368-375.

Ohio admitted as a free State, 1802.

Purchase of Louisiana 1803

"I have just given to England a maritime rival that will, sooner or later, humble her pride."
Bonaparte.

"For the first time in the national history, all parties agreed that the government could govern."
Adams.

- Adams, ii. 42-50, 95-134.
- Blaine, Twenty Years in Congress, i. 5-9.
- Bryant & Gay, iv. 145-149.
- Bryce, ii. 11.
- Coffin, Building the Nation, 120.
- Eggleston, 234, 235.
- Fiske, Hist. of U.S., 273, 274.
- Hart, Epochs Am. History, 185-187.
- Higginson, 244, 245.
- Hildreth, v. 478-481, 492, 493.
- Irving-Fiske, 523, 524.
- Johnston, Hist. Am. Politics, 57.
- Johnston, 167, 168.
- Lalor, Cyclopædia, i. 93-96.
- Lossing, Field Book, 132-134.
- McMaster, ii. 625-632; iii. 1-9.
- Montgomery, 204.
- Morse, Life of Jefferson, 250-258.
- Patton, i. 600, 601.
- Rhodes, i. 27, 28.
- Richardson, 298.
- Schouler, ii. 44-53.
- Sheldon-Barnes, 215-218.
- Smith, Goldwin, 158, 159.
- Thomas, 162.
- Von Holst, i. 183-192.
- Winsor, vii. 478, 479, 547.

Change in the Mode of Electing Presidents, and
- Adams, ii. 131-134.
- Eggleston, 227, 228.
- Fiske, Hist. of U.S., 270.

Handbook of American History

the Twelfth Amendment to the Constitution

See the American History Leaflets, No. 8, Text of Constitution.

- Hildreth, v. 506, 507.
- Johnston, Hist. Am. Politics, 58.
- Johnston, 148, 150, 164.
- Lalor, Cyclopædia, i. 608, 806, 807; ii. 135.
- McMaster, ii. 529, 530; iii. 183-187.
- Morse, Life of Jefferson, 206.
- Schouler, ii. 59, 60.
- Stanwood, Presidential Elections, 45-48.
- Thomas, 165.
- Winsor, vii. 269, 270.

Oregon Discovery and Lewis and Clarke Expedition

- Adams, iii. 12, 13, 215.
- H. H. Bancroft, Northwest Coast, ii. chs. 1-3.
- Barrows, Oregon, 57-63.
- Blaine, i. 12, 13.
- Bryant & Gay, iv. 170.
- Coffin, Building the Nation, 366, 367.
- Fiske, Hist. of U.S., 274. 275.
- Hart, Epochs Am. History, 233.
- Higginson, 245-247.
- Hildreth, v. 498.
- Irving-Fiske, 525.
- Johnston, 168, 241.
- Lalor, Cyclopædia, ii. 1046.
- McMaster, ii. 633-635; iii. 142-144.
- Montgomery, 205, 206.
- Richardson, 298-300.
- Schouler, ii. 130.
- Sheldon-Barnes, 217-219.
- Thomas, 163.
- Winsor, vii. 556, 557.

Duel of Burr and Hamilton

"In Hamilton's death, the Federalists and the country experienced a loss second

- Adams, ii. 186-191.
- Bryant & Gay, iv. 149.
- Bryce, ii. 7, 8.
- Coffin, Building the Nation, 133-138.
- Eggleston, 215.
- Hart, Epochs Am. History, 189.
- Higginson, 242.

Duel of Burr and Hamilton
(Continued)

only to that of Washington." *Hildreth.*

" Protection, force, and energy in the central government, financial stability, these are Hamilton's great legacy to the American Union." *Schouler.*

- Hildreth, v. 520-527.
- Irving-Fiske, 525, 526.
- Johnston, Hist. Am. Politics, 59.
- Johnston, 136.
- Lalor, Cyclopædia, i. 324.
- Lodge, Life of Hamilton, 237-252.
- Lossing, 134, 135.
- McMaster, iii. 52-54.
- Patton, i. 603-605.
- Richardson, 306, 307.
- Schouler, ii. 61-66.
- Thomas, 164, 165.

Second Administration of Thomas Jefferson 1805-1809.

Conspiracy of Aaron Burr

See Constitution Art. III. Sect. 3

- Adams, iii. 219-342.
- Bryant & Gay, iv. 149-153.
- Coffin, Building the Nation, 138, 139.
- Eggleston, 235.
- Fiske, Hist. of U.S., 276.
- Hart, Epochs Am. History, 189-191.
- Higginson, 242, 243.
- Hildreth, v. 594-624, 668-673.
- Irving-Fiske, 526.
- Johnston, Hist. Am. Politics, 63, 64.
- Johnston, 170.
- Lalor, Cyclopædia, i. 324.
- Lossing, 134-137.
- McMaster, iii. 55-88.
- Montgomery, 207.
- Morse, Life of Jefferson, 280-285.
- Parton, Life of Burr, ii. chs. 22-26.
- Patton, i. 605.
- Richardson, 307, 308.
- Schouler, ii. 118-124.
- Sheldon-Barnes, 283.
- Smith, Goldwin, 159.
- Stanwood, Presidential Elections, 48-50
- Thomas, 165.
- Winsor, vii. 338-340.

Fulton's "Clermont" 1807

- Adams, i. 69, 71, 182.
- Bryant & Gay, iv. 169, 170.
- Coffin, Building the Nation, 140, 141.
- Eggleston, 271, 272.
- Fiske, Hist. of U.S., 300.
- Higginson, 241, 242.
- Hildreth, v. 551.
- Irving-Fiske, 537.
- Johnston, 169.
- Lossing, Field Book, 242.
- McMaster, iii. 487-491.
- Montgomery, 208.
- Patton, ii. 687.
- Richardson, 308-311.
- Schouler, ii. 266, 267.
- Sheldon-Barnes, 283.
- Thomas, 169, 170.

Aggressions on Neutral Trade by England and France The Berlin and Milan Decrees and the British Orders in Council

- Adams, iii. 370-391; iv. 79-104.
- Bryant & Gay, iv. 172-175.
- Coffin, Building of the Nation, 142-144.
- Eggleston, 240.
- Fiske, Hist. of U.S., 277.
- Hart, Epochs Am. History, 191, 192.
- Higginson, 236.
- Hildreth, v. 646-649; vi. 33-35.
- Irving-Fiske, 526.
- Johnston, 171.
- Lalor, Cyclopædia, ii. 81.
- Lossing, 140-148.
- McMaster, iii. 249-251, 292, 293.
- Montgomery, 206.
- Morse, Life of Jefferson, 273-276.
- Patton, i. 607-610.
- Richardson, 314.
- Roosevelt, Naval War of 1812, 1-6.
- Schouler, ii. 151-156.
- Sheldon-Barnes, 230, 231.
- Smith, Goldwin, 161-164.
- Thomas, 166-168.

Period of Republican Supremacy

Aggressions etc.
(Continued)
- Von Holst, i. 200, 201.
- Winsor, vii. 481, 482.

Affair of the Leopard and Chesapeake
- Adams, iv. 1-26.
- Bryant & Gay, iv. 176, 177.
- Fiske, Hist. of U.S., 277.
- Hart, Epochs Am. History, 194.
- Higginson, 236.
- Hildreth, v. 678-682.
- Irving-Fiske, 527.
- Johnston, 172.
- Lalor, Cyclopædia, iii. 994.
- Lossing, 155-159.
- Maclay, Hist. U.S. Navy, i. 305-308.
- McMaster, iii. 253-262.
- Montgomery, 206.
- Morse, Life of Jefferson, 296-298.
- Patton, i. 610, 611.
- Richardson, 315.
- Roosevelt, The Naval War of 1812, 6, 7.
- Schouler, ii. 145-147.
- Sheldon-Barnes, 231.
- Thomas, 167, 168.

The Embargo Act in force 1 year 3 months

"The one stern measure of this eight-years administration."
- Adams, iv. 152-177, 249-289.
- Bryant & Gay, iv. 178, 179.
- Coffin, Building the Nation, 143.
- Eggleston, 241.
- Fiske, Hist. of U.S., 278.
- Gay, Life of Madison, 264-282.
- Hart, Epochs Am. History, 195-198.
- Higginson, 236.
- Hildreth, vi. 36-44, 69, 84-87, 110-128.
- Irving-Fiske, 526-528.
- Johnston, Hist. Am. Politics, 65, 66.
- Johnston, 172.
- Lalor, Cyclopædia, ii. 81-85.
- Lossing, 162, 163.
- McMaster, iii. 449-451.
- Montgomery, 209.

The Embargo Act in force 1 year 3 months
(Continued)

- Morse, Life of Jefferson, 298-312.
- Patton, i. 612, 613.
- Schouler, ii. 151, 156-165, 173-178.
- Sheldon-Barnes, 230.
- Smith, Goldwin, 164, 165.
- Thomas, 168.
- Von Holst, i. 200-210, 216, 217.
- Winsor, vii. 274, 482.

Foreign Slave Trade Forbidden 1808

See Text of Constitution Art. I. Sect. 9

- Adams, iii. 347, 357-361.
- Greeley, Am. Conflict, i. 66, 67.
- Hart, Epochs Am. History, 237.
- Higginson, 240.
- Hildreth, vi. 638, 661, 701.
- Irving-Fiske, 555.
- Johnston, Hist. Am. Politics, 11.
- Johnston, 141, 167.
- Lalor, Cyclopædia, iii. 732.
- McMaster, iii. 520, 521.
- Montgomery, 209.
- Schouler, ii. 125-128.
- Sheldon-Barnes, 223, 224.
- Thomas, 166, and Note.
- Von Holst, i. 293-298, 317.
- Winsor, vii. 291, 292.

Retirement of Jefferson His Character

"His character has contributed most strongly in forming that of his country: Liberal education, liberal religion, a free press, America for the Americans, all these things are Jeffersonian."

- Adams, iv. 454-474.
- Bryant & Gay, iv. 164-166, 168, 180.
- Coffin, Building the Nation, 119.
- Eggleston, 172, 200.
- Fiske, Hist. of U.S., 271, 272.
- Hart, Epochs Am. History, 177-179, 198, 222.
- Higginson, 235.
- Hildreth, vi. 138-143.
- Johnston, 166.
- Lalor, Clyclopædia, ii. 639.
- McMaster, iii. 336.
- Montgomery, 201, 202.
- Morse, Life of Jefferson, 331-344.

Period of Republican Supremacy

Retirement of Jefferson etc.
(Continued)

- Richardson, 406.
- Schouler, ii. 198-204.
- Von Holst, i. 159, 160, 191, 192.

Election and Inauguration of James Madison

"Washington, who ruled superior to party, Adams, who ruled in spite of a party, Jefferson, who ruled at the head of a party, Madison, the first of the Presidents who have been the exponents of a party."

- Adams, v. 1-12.
- Bryant & Gay, iv. 180, 181.
- Coffin, Building the Nation, 144.
- Eggleston, 241, 242.
- Fiske, Hist. of U.S., 278.
- Gay, Life of Madison, 283.
- Hart, Epochs Am. History, 200.
- Higginson, 248.
- Hildreth, vi. 95, 149, 150.
- Johnston, Hist. Am. Politics, 68.
- Johnston, 174.
- Lossing, 169, 175.
- McMaster, iii. 317, 318, 336, 337.
- Montgomery, 210.
- Schouler, ii. 183, 184, 279, 280.
- Stanwood, Presidential Elections, 51-56.
- Thomas, 169.

Summary of the Period of Republican Supremacy 1801-1809

1801
: Jefferson Inaugurated.
: Barbary Wars and Decatur's Exploit.

1802
: Ohio Admitted.

1803
: Purchase of Louisiana.
: The Twelfth Constitutional Amendment.

1804
: Oregon Discovery, and Lewis and Clark Expedition.
: Duel of Burr and Hamilton.

1805
: Jefferson's Second Term Begins.

1806
: The Berlin Decree by Napoleon.

1807	Conspiracy of Aaron Burr. Fulton's Clermont. Milan Decree by Napoleon. British Orders in Council. Affair of the Leopard and Chesapeake. The Embargo Act.
1808	Foreign Slave Trade Forbidden.
1809	Retirement of Jefferson. Inauguration of James Madison.

The Period of Foreign War

First Administration of James Madison 1809-1813

Tecumseh and Tippecanoe
- Adams, vi. 90-112.
- Bryant & Gay, iv. 182, 183.
- Coffin, Building the Nation, 145, 146.
- Eggleston, 242.
- Fiske, Hist. of U.S., 285.
- Higginson, 249.
- Hildreth, vi. 251-259.
- Irving-Fiske, 529, 533.
- Johnston, 175, 179
- Lossing, 194-209.
- McMaster, iii. 529-536.
- Montgomery, 211.
- Patton, ii. 619-621.
- Richardson, 312, 313.
- Schouler, ii. 331-335.
- Sheldon-Barnes, 284.
- Thomas, 170.
- Winsor, vii. 375, 376.

Louisiana, the eighteenth State, admitted to the Union, 1812.

Causes of the War of 1812

1. British Tampering with Indians.
2. Orders in Council.
3. Interference with Commerce.
4. Impressment of American seamen.
5. The Chesapeake Outrage.

- Adams, vi. 116, 117, 221, 323.
- Bryant & Gay, iv. 181, 185, 186.
- Coffin, Building the Nation, 142-144, 147, 148.
- Cooper, Naval Hist., ii. 14-18, 22, 23.
- Fiske, Hist. of U.S., 279-280.
- Gay, Life of Madison, 301-312.
- Hart, Epochs Am. History, 203-206.
- Higginson, 248.
- Hildreth, vi. 313-317.
- Irving-Fiske, 529.
- Lalor, Cyclopædia, ii. 81, 82.

Causes of the War of 1812
(Continued)

How is war declared?
See Constitution Art. I. Sect. 8

- Lossing, 226, 227, 247.
- McMaster, iii. 253, 456, 457.
- Montgomery, 211, 212.
- Patton, ii. 632.
- Richardson, 314-316.
- Roosevelt, Naval War of 1812, 1-8.
- Schouler, ii. 144-153, 334, 346, 355.
- Schurz, Life of Clay, i. 67-77.
- Sheldon-Barnes, 230, 231.
- Smith, Goldwin, 165-170.
- Thomas, 171.
- Von Holst, Life of Calhoun, 12-15.
- Von Holst, i. 222-238.
- Winsor, vii. 376.

Campaign of 1812 on Land

Hull's Surrender. Battle of Queenstown.

- Adams, vi. 296-300, 312-335.
- Bryant & Gay, iv. 187-190.
- Coffin, Building the Nation, 153-158.
- Eggleston, 245.
- Fiske, Hist. of U.S., 285.
- Hart, Epochs Am. History, 209.
- Higginson, 249.
- Hildreth, vi. 335-342, 355-359, 362-364.
- Irving-Fiske, 532, 533.
- Johnston, 177, 178.
- Lossing, 260-289, 381-432.
- McMaster, iii. 556-560.
- Montgomery, 212-213.
- Patton, ii. 630, 631.
- Richardson, 316-320.
- Roosevelt, pp. xiii., xiv.
- Schouler, ii. 357, 358, 359-361.
- Thomas, 173.
- Winsor, vii. 382-385.

The Year 1812 upon the Sea

Four Great Ship Duels.

- Adams, vi. 373-387.
- Bryant and Gay, iv. 192, 193.
- Coffin, Building the Nation, 159-170.
- Cooper, Naval Hist., ii. 55-59.
- Eggleston, 246, 247.

The Period of Foreign War

The Year 1812 upon the Sea
(Continued)

Holmes' "*Old Ironsides.*"

- Fiske, Hist. of U.S., 281–284.
- Hart, Epochs Am. History, 210.
- Higginson, 249.
- Hildreth, vi. 367-370.
- Irving-Fiske, 530.
- Johnston, 181, 182.
- Lossing, Field Book, 441-462.
- Maclay, Hist. of U.S. Navy, i. 344-360, 364-384, 401-411.
- McMaster, iv.
- Montgomery, 213, 214.
- Patton, ii. 637-641.
- Richardson, 320-324.
- Roosevelt, 89-97, 100-105, 108-114, 119-127.
- Schouler, ii. 362, 363.
- Sheldon-Barnes, 232.
- Winsor, vii. 380-382.

Second Administration of James Madison 1813-1817

Campaign of 1813 on Land

Battle of the Thames.
Death of Tecumseh.

- Bryant & Gay, iv. 199, 200.
- Coffin, Building the Nation, 194.
- Eggleston, 251, 252.
- Hart, Epochs Am. History, 209, 210.
- Higginson, 249.
- Hildreth, vi. 437, 438.
- Irving-Fiske, 533.
- Johnston, 179.
- Lossing, 551-559.
- McMaster, iv.
- Patton, ii. 647.
- Richardson, 331.
- Schouler, ii. 385.
- Winsor, vii. 392.

The Year 1813 upon the Sea

Loss of the Chesapeake.

- Bryant & Gay, iv. 191, 192, 198, 199, 206, 207.
- Coffin, Building the Nation, 178, 179, 187-193.

The Year 1813 upon the Sea
(Continued)

Cruise of the Essex.
Perry's Victory on Lake Erie.
"We have met the enemy, and they are ours."
Commodore Perry.

- Eggleston, 248, 249.
- Fiske, Hist. of U.S., 285, 286.
- Hart, Epochs Am. History, 209, 211.
- Higginson, 249, 250.
- Hildreth, vi. 411, 420-422, 430, 435-437, 486.
- Irving-Fiske, 531, 533.
- Johnston, 183-185, 187, 188.
- Lossing, 518-533, 703-709, 721-733.
- Maclay, Hist. U.S. Navy, i. 436-459, 492-517, 542-575.
- McMaster, iv.
- Montgomery, 214.
- Patton, ii. 645, 646.
- Richardson, 327-331.
- Roosevelt, 78-81, 254-273, 291-300.
- Schouler, ii. 383-385, 392-394.
- Sheldon, 234.
- Thomas, 173.
- Winsor, vii. 386, 387, 391, 392, 395.

Campaign of 1814 on Land

Battle of Chippewa.
Battle of Lundy's Lane.
Attack on Baltimore.
Capture of Washington.
"Star-Spangled Banner."

- Bryant & Gay, iv. 211-214, 217-222.
- Coffin, Building the Nation, 196-200, 212-219.
- Eggleston, 252, 253.
- Fiske, Hist. of U.S., 287.
- Hart, Epochs Am. History, 213.
- Higginson, 251.
- Hildreth, vi. 492-497, 501-512, 517-518.
- Irving-Fiske, 533, 534.
- Johnston, 190-193.
- Lossing, Field Book, 804-815, 816-824.
- McMaster, iv.
- Montgomery, 216, 217.
- Patton, ii. 662-665, 668-672.
- Richardson, 332, 333.
- Schouler, ii. 403-406, 407-412.
- Smith, Goldwin, 171.
- Thomas, 175, 176.
- Winsor, vii. 393, 394, 400-403.

The Period of Foreign War   31

The Year 1814 upon the Lakes

MacDonough's Victory.

"Down to the time of our Civil War he is the greatest figure in our Naval History."
Roosevelt.

- Bryant & Gay, iv. 214-216.
- Coffin, Building the Nation, 203-205.
- Cooper, Naval Hist., 212-224.
- Eggleston, 249.
- Hart, Epochs Am. History, 213.
- Hildreth, vi. 518, 519.
- Irving-Fiske, 534.
- Johnston, 188, 189.
- Lossing, 865-873.
- Maclay, Hist. of the Navy, ii.
- McMaster, iv.
- Montgomery, 217.
- Patton, ii. 666.
- Richardson, 340.
- Roosevelt, 375-398.
- Schouler, ii. 406.
- Thomas, 175.
- Winsor, vii. 397-400.

Dissatisfaction in New England

The Hartford Convention.

- Bryant & Gay, iv. 229-233, 239.
- Bryce, Am. Com., ii. 10.
- Benton, Thirty Years' View, i. 4.
- Coffin, Building the Nation, 223.
- Fiske, Hist. of U.S., 288.
- Greeley, Am. Conflict, i. 85, 86.
- Hart, Epochs Am. History, 214-218.
- Higginson, 249.
- Hildreth, vi. 530-536.
- Irving-Fiske, 535.
- Johnston, Hist. Am. Politics, 78, 79.
- Johnston, 192.
- Lalor, Cyclopædia, i. 624-626.
- Lossing, 1012-1016.
- McMaster, iv.
- Montgomery, 219, Note.
- Patton, ii. 672-676.
- Schouler, ii. 417, 424-430.
- Sheldon, 237, 238.
- Smith, Goldwin, 171.
- Thomas, 177.

Dissatisfaction etc.
(*Continued*)

{ Von Holst, i. 260-272.
Winsor, vii. 252, 253, 277, 321.

Jackson's Victory at New Orleans Jan. 8, 1815

"History records no example of so glorious a victory obtained with so little bloodshed on the part of the victorious." *Monroe.*

"The only military achievement of this war which left upon Europe a memorable impression." *Schouler.*

{ Bryant & Gay, iv. 233-236.
Coffin, Building the Nation, 225-231.
Eggleston, 254.
Fiske, Hist. of U.S., 288.
Hart, Epochs Am. History, 214.
Higginson, 251.
Hildreth, vi. 557-566.
Irving-Fiske, 534, 535.
Johnston, 195, 196.
Lossing, 1023-1050.
McMaster, iv.
Montgomery, 218, 219.
Morse, Life of Jackson, i. 36-48.
Parton, Life of Jackson, ii. 186-213.
Patton, ii. 677-681.
Richardson, 341-344.
Roosevelt, 455-493.
Schouler, ii. 413, 414, 438-443.
Schurz, Life of Clay, i. 117, 118.
Sheldon, 235, 236.
Smith, Goldwin, 172, 173.
Thomas, 177, 178.
Winsor, vii. 403, 404.

Close of the War

Treaty of Ghent

Effects of the War:
1. National Pride.
2. Training of Soldiers.
3. Freedom from European Politics.
4. Disappearance of the Federalist Party.
5. Gain in the spirit of Nationality.

{ Bryant & Gay, iv. 236, 238-242.
Coffin, Building the Nation, 228-231.
Eggleston, 254, 255.
Fiske, Hist. of U.S., 289.
Hart, Epochs Am. History, 218, 222.
Haswell, Treaties and Conventions, 399-405.
Higginson, 251, 252.
Hildreth, vi. 565-569.
Irving-Fiske, 535.
Johnston, Hist. Am. Politics, 77, 78, 80.
Johnston, 196.
Lalor, Cyclopædia, iii. 946, 1090.

The Period of Foreign War

Close of the War Treaty of Ghent
(*Continued*)

"It will be seen that the treaty did not touch one of the points on which the United States had declared war."
Johnston.

- Lossing, 1060-1067.
- McMaster, iv.
- Montgomery, 219.
- Morse, Life of John Q. Adams, 75-98.
- Morse, Life of Albert Gallatin, 312-340.
- Patton, ii. 682, 683.
- Richardson, 344.
- Roosevelt, 400.
- Schouler, ii. 431-437.
- Schurz, Life of Clay, i. 102-125.
- Sheldon, 236.
- Smith, Goldwin, 172.
- Von Holst, i. 273-275.
- Winsor, vii. 483-488.

The Algerine War and Subjection of the Barbary States

"The Americans have done more for Christendom against the pirates of Africa than all the powers of Europe united."
Pope Pius VII.

- Bryant & Gay, iv. 243, 244.
- Cooper, Naval History, iii. 7-15.
- Eggleston, 229.
- Fiske, Hist. of U.S., 275, 276.
- Hart, Epochs Am. History, 232.
- Hildreth, vi. 577, 578.
- Johnston, 199.
- Lalor, Cyclopædia, i. 56.
- Maclay, History U.S. Navy, ii.
- Patton, ii. 685.
- Richardson, 344, 345.
- Schouler, ii. 455, 456.
- Winsor, vii. 405, 406.

The First Protective Tariff

Enacted April 27, 1816
Introduced the two new principles of *protection* and *specific duties*.

- Blaine, i. 190.
- Bryant & Gay, iv. 244, 245.
- Coffin, Building the Nation, 247.
- Fiske, Hist. of U.S., 306, 307.
- Greeley, Am. Conflict, i. 90.
- Hart, Epochs Am. History, 229-231.
- Higginson, 261, 262.
- Hildreth, vi. 585-588.
- Irving-Fiske, 541.
- Johnston, Hist. Am. Politics, 81.
- Johnston, 198.

34 Handbook of American History

The First Protective Tariff *(Continued)*
{
Lalor, Cyclopædia, i. 773; iii. 859, 860.
Montgomery, 219, 240, Note.
Patton, ii. 686.
Richardson, 358, 359.
Schouler, ii. 450.
Sheldon, 238, 239.
Smith, Goldwin, 185.
Taussig, Tariff History of U.S., 16-19, 63, 68, 69.
Thomas, 185, 186.
Von Holst, i. 398-400.
Winsor, vii. 278.
}

Indiana, the nineteenth State, admitted, 1816.
The first ocean steamer, the Savannah, crosses the Atlantic, 1819.

Election of the Fifth President James Monroe
{
Bryant & Gay, iv. 246..
Coffin, Building the Nation, 232.
Eggleston, 264.
Fiske, Hist. of U.S., 298.
Hart, Epochs Am. History, 231, 232.
Higginson, 253.
Hildreth, vi. 593, 595.
Irving-Fiske, 535, 536.
Johnston, Hist. Am. Politics, 81, 83.
Johnston, 201.
Lalor, Cyclopædia, ii. 898.
Montgomery, 220.
Richardson, 345.
Sargent, Public Men and Events, i. 18, 19.
Schouler, ii. 458-461.
Sheldon, 285.
Smith, Goldwin, 175.
Stanwood, Pres. Elections, 64-69.
Thomas, 181.
Winsor, vii. 279.
}

Mississippi, the twentieth State, admitted, 1817.

Summary of the Period of Foreign War

1811	Tecumseh and Tippecanoe.
1812	Louisiana Admitted. War Declared against Great Britain. Causes of the War. Hull's Surrender, Aug. 16. Battle of Queenstown, Oct. 13. Four Great Ship Duels.
1813	Battle of the Thames, Oct. 5. Death of Tecumseh. The Loss of the Chesapeake. The Cruise of the Essex. Perry's Victory on Lake Erie, Sept. 10.
1814	Battle of Chippewa, July 5. Battle of Lundy's Lane, July 25. Attack on Baltimore. Capture of Washington, Aug. 24. McDonough's Victory on Lake Champlain, Sept. 11. Dissatisfaction in New England, and The Hartford Convention. Treaty of Peace Signed, Dec. 24.
1815	Jackson's Victory at New Orleans, Jan. 8. The Algerine War, and Subjection of the Barbary States.
1816	The First Protective Tariff. Indiana Admitted. National Bank Chartered.

Period of National Growth 1817–1829

First Administration of James Monroe 1817-1821

Beginnings of the Slavery Agitation

The three Compromises with Slavery in the Constitution.
1. Sect. 2. Apportionment of Representatives.
2. Art. I. Sect. 1. Limitation of the Slave Trade.
3. Art. IV. Sect. 2. Rendition of Fugitive Slaves.

See Text of Constitution.

- Blaine, i. 21-23.
- Bryant & Gay, iv. 260-265.
- Coffin, Building the Nation, 243.
- Eggleston, 259, 260.
- Fiske, Hist. of U.S., 300–302.
- Greeley, Am. Conflict, i. 66-74.
- Hart, Epochs Am. History, 236-238.
- Higginson, 254-256.
- Hildreth, vi. 635-638, 662-665.
- Irving-Fiske, 537, 538.
- Johnston, Hist. Am. Politics, 86.
- Johnston, 204.
- Lalor, Cyclopædia, i. 549-551, 774.
- Montgomery, 222-224.
- Patton, ii. 692-695.
- Richardson, 408.
- Schouler, iii. 100-103, 134-147.
- Sheldon, 242-244.
- Smith, Goldwin, 177-178.
- Thomas, 188.
- Von Holst, i. 350-360.
- Winsor, vii. 279, 280.

Illinois, the twenty-first State, admitted, 1818.
Alabama, the twenty-second State, admitted, 1819.

The Missouri Compromise

The three lines of division between slave and free territory.
1. Mason and Dixon's.

- Benton, Thirty Years' View, i. 8-10.
- Blaine, i. 16-21.
- Bryant & Gay, iv. 267-274.
- Bryce, Am. Commonwealth, ii. 12.
- Coffin, Building the Nation, 243.
- Eggleston, 259-261.
- Fiske, Hist. of U.S., 303.

Period of National Growth

The Missouri Compromise
(Continued)

2. The Ohio River.
3. The line of the Compromise, 36° 30'

- Gilman, Life of Monroe, 144-149.
- Greeley, Am. Conflict, i. 74-80.
- Hart, Epochs Am. History, 238-241.
- Higginson, 256.
- Hildreth, vi. 663, 664, 688-696.
- Irving-Fiske, 538, 539.
- Johnston, Hist. Am. Politics, 86, 88, 90.
- Johnston, 204, 205.
- Lalor, Cyclopædia, i. 549, 550; ii. 813.
- Missouri, Am. Commonwealths, 139-162.
- Montgomery, 225, 226.
- Patton, ii. 695.
- Richardson, 408.
- Schouler, iii. 164-173, 178-186.
- Schurz, Life of Clay, i. 172-198.
- Sheldon-Barnes, 241, 242.
- Smith, Goldwin, 177, 178.
- Thomas, 189.
- Von Holst, i. 373-382.
- Wilson, Rise and Fall of Slave Power, i. 145-149.
- Winsor, vii. 280, 281.

Maine, the twenty-third State, admitted, 1820.

The Seminole War

Seminoles, *i.e.*, "wanderers" refugee Creeks.

- Bryant & Gay, iv. 246-256.
- Coffin, Building the Nation, 242.
- Fiske, Hist. of U.S., 298.
- Gilman, Life of Monroe, 140, 141.
- Higginson, 253, 263, 264.
- Hildreth, vi. 641-646.
- Irving-Fiske, 536.
- Johnston, 202.
- Lalor, Cyclopædia, iii. 732.
- Montgomery, 221, 222.
- Patton, ii. 690-692.
- Richardson, 346.
- Sargent, Public Men and Events, i. 21, 22.
- Schouler, iii. 57-61, 69-75, 87-89.
- Sheldon, 285, 287.
- Sumner, Life of Jackson, 52-61.

The Seminole War (*Continued*)	Thomas, 184. Von Holst, i. 336-339. Winsor, vii. 406.
Temporary Settlement of the Northwest Boundary	Blaine, i. 48. Gilman, Life of Monroe, 249. Hart, Epochs Am. History, 233. Haswell, Treaties and Conventions, 415-418. Hildreth, vi. 659, 660. Lalor, Cyclopædia, ii. 1045, 1046. Schouler, iii. 330, 331. Winsor, vii. 491.
Purchase of Florida Possession given 1821 $5,000,000.00 For text of treaty with Spain, see Haswell, "Treaties and Conventions" 1016-1022 "It was an investment in swamps, everglades, and sandy barrens," but gave the U.S. control of the Gulf and the free navigation of the lower Mississippi.	Blaine, i. 13, 14. Bryant & Gay, iv. 259. Coffin, Building the Nation, 242, 243. Eggleston, 264. Fiske, Hist. of U.S., 299. Gilman, Life of Monroe, 143. Hart, Epochs Am. History, 233, 234. Higginson, 253, 254. Hildreth, vi. 658, 686, 713. Irving-Fiske, 536. Johnston, Hist. Am. Politics, 85. Johnston, 201, 202. Lalor, Cyclopædia, i. 96. Montgomery, 222. Patton, ii. 691, 692. Richardson, 346, 347. Schouler, iii. 95, 189. Schurz, Life of Clay, i. 162-165. Sheldon, 285. Thomas, 184, 185. Von Holst, i. 335, 336. Winsor, vii. 497-500.

Missouri, the twenty-fourth State, admitted, 1821.

Period of National Growth

Second Administration of James Monroe 1821-1825

The "Era of Good Feeling"

"No one but Washington was ever re-elected to the highest office in the land with so near an approach to unanimity."
Gilman.

- Bryant & Gay, iv. 277.
- Eggleston, 264.
- Fiske, Hist. of U.S., 297.
- Gilman, Life of Monroe, 12.
- Hart, Epochs Am. History, 249.
- Higginson, 253, 255.
- Hildreth, vi. 623.
- Irving-Fiske, 535, 536.
- Johnston, Hist. Am. Politics, 92.
- Johnston, 201.
- Lalor, Cyclopædia, ii. 108, 109.
- Montgomery, 221.
- Patton, ii. 689.
- Schouler, iii. 335, 336.
- Smith, Goldwin, 177.
- Stanwood, Presidential Elections, 70.
- Thomas, 183.
- Von Holst, i. 382.
- Winsor, vii. 279.

The "American System" or System of Internal Improvements and Protective Duties

Cumberland Road, extended from Cumberland, Md., to the West, and finally reached Illinois.
1. To establish post-offices and post-roads.
2. To declare war.
3. To regulate commerce between the States.

- Bryant & Gay, iv. 274.
- Eggleston, 272, 273.
- Fiske, Hist. of U.S., 305-307.
- Gilman, Life of Monroe, 149, 248.
- Hart, Epochs of Am. History, 224, 227-229, 253, 254.
- Higginson, 260.
- Hildreth, vi. 591, 592, 616, 617, 624.
- Irving-Fiske, 541.
- Johnston, 206, 207, 211.
- Lalor, Cyclopædia, ii. 568-572.
- Montgomery, 226, 227.
- Patton, ii. 700.
- Sargent, Public Men and Events, i. 25-28.

The "American System" etc.
(Continued)

4. To provide for the general welfare.
5. To regulate territory and property of the U.S.

These are the powers of the Constitution by which the right to make internal improvements is claimed.

What is the so-called "Elastic Clause" of the Constitution?

Schouler, iii. 54, 55, 247-254, 295, 296.
Schurz, Life of Clay, i. 40, 145, 146.
Thomas, 186, 187.
Von Holst, i. 388-394.
Winsor, vii. 274, 275, 279.

The Erie Canal

"Three hundred sixty-three miles long; surmounts a rise of 600 feet; completed fifty years from the date of Battle of Bunker Hill."

Bryant & Gay, iv. 275.
Coffin, Building the Nation, 238-242.
Eggleston, 272, 273.
Fiske, Hist. of U.S., 306.
Higginson, 260.
Hildreth, vi. 624, 625.
Irving-Fiske, 539.
Johnston, 206.
Lalor, Cyclopædia, i. 339.
Montgomery, 229-231.
Patton, ii. 700.
Sargent, Public Men and Events, i. 97-100.
Schouler, iii. 232, 346-348.
Sheldon, 285.
Thomas, 187.
Von Holst, i. 393.

Clay's Tariff of 1824

"The Act of 1824 opened the struggle between Free Trade and Protection."

Blaine, i. 191.
Bryant & Gay, iv. 278.
Fiske, Hist. of U.S., 308.
Hart, Epochs Am. History, 247, 248.
Higginson, 261, 262.
Johnston, Hist. Am. Politics, 94.
Johnston, 207.
Lalor, Cyclopædia, iii. 860, 861.

Period of National Growth

Clay's Tariff of 1824
(Continued)

- Lodge, Life of Daniel Webster, 163-165.
- Patton, ii. 697.
- Schouler, iii. 296-298.
- Schurz, Life of Clay, i. 212-220.
- Smith, Goldwin, 185-188.
- Sumner, Life of Jackson, 198-200.
- Taussig, Tariff Hist. of U.S., 74-78.
- Thomas, 191.
- Von Holst, i. 401-405.

Visit of Lafayette

- Coffin, Building the Nation, 245-246.
- Gilman, Life of Monroe, 250, 251.
- Higginson, 256.
- Johnston, 205, 206.
- Montgomery, 228.
- Patton, ii. 697, 698.
- Richardson, 347.
- Sargent, Public Men and Events, i. 89-95.
- Schouler, iii. 316-324, 328, 352.
- Schurz, Life of Clay, i. 234, 235.
- Thomas, 194-196.

The Monroe Doctrine

Included in the President's annual message to Congress, 1823.

John Quincy Adams the real author of this doctrine.

- Bryant & Gay, iv. 279, 285.
- Coffin, Building the Nation, 244, 245.
- Eggleston, 265.
- Fiske, Hist. of U.S., 299.
- Gilman, Life of Monroe, 156-174.
- Hart, Epochs Am. History, 243, 244.
- Higginson, 258.
- Johnston, Hist. American Politics, 93.
- Johnston, 205.
- Lalor, Cyclopædia, ii. 898-900.
- Montgomery, 227, 228.
- Patton, ii. 696.
- Richardson, 348.
- Schouler, iii. 287-292, 362.
- Smith, Goldwin, 175, 176.
- Thomas, 190, 191.
- Von Holst, i. 420, 421.
- Winsor, vii. 281, 502, 524.

Election of the Sixth President John Quincy Adams

"To glance at a good portrait of this man is to feel positive that he had his opinion and was prepared to state it."

Election by the House of Representatives, from the three highest candidates, Jackson, Adams, Crawford.

See Const., XIIth Amendment.

"This election gave the death-blow to the custom of nominating candidates by a caucus held by members of Congress."
Patton.

Bryant & Gay, iv. 280, 281.
Eggleston, 265.
Fiske, Hist. of U.S., 304.
Hart, Epochs Am. History, 250, 251.
Higginson, 259.
Irving-Fiske, 540.
Johnston, Hist. Am. Politics, 96, 97.
Johnston, 207, 208.
Lalor, Cyclopædia, i. 24.
Montgomery, 229.
Morse, Life of Adams, 169-178.
Patton, ii. 698.
Richardson, 348.
Sargent, Public Men and Events, i. 75, 79.
Schouler, iii. 324, 329, 397-409.
Smith, Goldwin, 191-195.
Stanwood, Presidential Elections, 79, 95.
Thomas, 192, 193.
Winsor, vii. 282.

Administration of John Quincy Adams 1825-1829

Attempt at a Panama Congress

Benton, Thirty Years' View, i. 65, 69.
Bryant & Gay, iv. 283, 284.
Greeley, Am. Conflict, i. 267, 268.
Hart, Epochs Am. History, 251-253.
Morse, Life of John Quincy Adams, 190, 191.
Sargent, Public Men and Events, i. 105, 115-117.
Schouler, iii. 358-365.
Thomas, 197.
Von Holst, i. 409-413.
Winsor, vii. 503.

Period of National Growth

**Georgia and the Creek Indians
A Conflict of State and National Authority**

"The political importance of the case lay in the fact that its result was the first successful nullification, in its modern sense, of the laws of the United States."
Johnston.

- Benton, Thirty Years' View, i. 27-29.
- Bryant & Gay, iv. 287-289.
- Greeley, 102-106.
- Hart, Epochs Am. History, 255, 256.
- Johnston, 210, 211.
- Lalor, Cyclopædia, i. 391-394.
- Patton, ii. 700, 701, 706.
- Sargent, Public Men and Events, i. 96, 97, 104, 135-137.
- Schouler, iii. 370-373, 378-383.
- Sumner, Life of Jackson, 181-183.
- Thomas, 197, 198.
- Von Holst, i. 433-437.
- Wilson, Epochs Am. History, 35-38.
- Winsor, vii. 286.

Deaths of Adams and Jefferson July 4, 1826

"On the fiftieth anniversary of the Declaration of Independence, of which Jefferson was author and Adams principal supporter."
Johnston.

"The tears which flow and the honors which are paid when the founders of the republic die, give hope that the republic itself may be immortal."
Webster.

- Benton, Thirty Years' View, i. 87, 88.
- Eggleston, 172, 221.
- Hart, Epochs Am. History, 245.
- Higginson, 261.
- Johnston, 211.
- Lalor, Cyclopædia, i. 24.
- Lodge, Life of Webster, 125, 126.
- Morse, Life of John Adams, 330.
- Patton, ii. 701, 702.
- Richardson, 348, 351.
- Sargent, Public Men and Events, i. 131.
- Schouler, iii. 386, 387.
- Thomas, 199.
- Winsor, vii. 307.

Methods of Presidential Nominations

1789–1800. No formal nominations.
1800–1824. By Congressional caucuses.
1824–1840. By State legislatures and popular assemblies.

1840 to the present. By party conventions.
See Bryce, Am. Commonwealths, Vol. ii. 172.

Tariff of 1828

"Called by its enemies 'The Tariff of Abominations.'"
Fiske.

"The highest and most protective ever adopted in this country." *Greeley.*

- Benton, Thirty Years' View, i. 95-102.
- Blaine, i. 191, 192.
- Bryant & Gay, iv. 291.
- Fiske, Hist. of U.S., 308.
- Greeley, Am. Conflict, i. 91, 92.
- Hart, Epochs Am. History, 257, 258.
- Higginson, 261, 262.
- Irving-Fiske, 541, 542.
- Johnston, Hist. Am. Politics, 100.
- Johnston, 212.
- Lalor, Cyclopædia, iii. 861, 862.
- Lodge, Life of Webster, 154-168.
- Montgomery, 240, 241.
- Patton, ii. 702-704.
- Rhodes, Hist. United States, i. 40, 41.
- Sargent, Public Men and Events, i. 148.
- Schouler, iii. 420-426.
- Smith, Goldwin, 188, 189.
- Sumner, Life of Jackson, 200-206.
- Taussig, Tariff History of U.S., 89-101.
- Thomas, 199, 200.
- Von Holst, i. 402-408, 459.

Election of the Seventh President Andrew Jackson

"The Era of People Worship, as though ignorance and passion, multiplied a million times, could be divine."
Goldwin Smith.

- Bryant & Gay, iv. 295, 296.
- Bryce, Am. Commonwealth, ii. 172.
- Coffin, Building the Nation, 247.
- Eggleston, 266.
- Fiske, Hist. of U.S., 308.
- Greeley, Am. Conflict, i. 88, 89.
- Hart, Epochs Am. History, 261.
- Higginson, 262.
- Irving-Fiske, 540.
- Johnston, Hist. Am. Politics, 101-103.
- Johnston, 212-214.
- Lalor, Cyclopædia, ii. 626.
- Montgomery, 234, 235.
- Patton, ii. 704.
- Richardson, 352, 353.

Election of the Seventh President Andrew Jackson
(Continued)

"It was the People's Day, the People's President, and the People would rule."

Von Holst.

{ Sargent, Public Men and Events, i. 151, 162-164.
Schouler, iii. 437, 438, 451-453.
Sheldon, 286.
Smith, Goldwin, 195.
Stanwood, Presidential Elections, 96-101.
Sumner, Life of Jackson, 114-118.
Thomas, 200.
Von Holst, ii. 2-6, 11.
Wilson, Epochs Am. History, 19-21.
Winsor, vii. 283, 348. }

Summary of the Period of National Growth 1817-1829

1817
: Monroe Inaugurated.
  Mississippi Admitted.
  Beginnings of the Slavery Agitation.

1818
: Illinois Admitted.

1819
: Alabama Admitted.
  Treaty for the Annexation of Florida.

1820
: Maine Admitted.
  The Missouri Compromise.
  The Seminole War.

1821
: Missouri Admitted.
  Monroe's Second Term.
  Purchase of Florida.
  Temporary Settlement of the Northwest Boundary.

1822
: Internal Improvements and Protective Duties.
  The Era of Good Feeling.

1823
: The Monroe Doctrine.

1824
: Clay's Tariff.
  Visit of Lafayette.
  Election of John Quincy Adams.

1825	{ The Erie Canal. Inauguration of John Quincy Adams. Attempt at a Panama Congress.
1826	Deaths of Adams and Jefferson, July 4.
1827	Georgia and the Creek Indian Troubles.
1828	{ A New Protective Tariff. Formation of the Whig and Democratic Parties. Election of Andrew Jackson. The First Locomotive Imported from England.

Period of Critical Change

PERIOD OF CRITICAL CHANGE 1829–1842

First Administration of Andrew Jackson 1829-1833

The "Kitchen Cabinet"

"Back of the Cabinet there still stood the 'Kitchen Cabinet,' which always possessed undue power, and was the deciding influence in the most important questions." *Von Holst.*

- Bryant & Gay, iv. 298.
- Lalor, Cyclopædia, ii. 677.
- Parton, Life of Jackson, iii. 178.
- Sargent, Public Men and Events, i. 152-157, 164, 184, 185.
- Schouler, iii. 495.
- Smith, Goldwin, 197.
- Sumner, Life of Jackson, 140-145.
- Thomas, 204.
- Von Holst, ii. 27, 28.
- Wilson, Epochs Am. History, 28-30.

The Webster-Hayne Debate

Foote's resolution regarding the sale of the public lands the occasion.

- Benton, Thirty Years' View, i. 138-142, 337-342.
- Bryant & Gay, iv. 305, 306.
- Coffin, Building the Nation, 248, 249.
- Fiske, Hist. of U.S., 310.
- Irving-Fiske, 543.
- Johnston, 228.
- Lalor, Cyclopædia, ii. 234, 1052; iii. 1098.
- Lodge, Life of Webster, 172-204.
- Montgomery, 241, 242.
- Patton, ii. 722.
- Rhodes, i. 42.
- Richardson, 363.
- Sargent, Public Men and Events, i. 170-174.
- Schouler, iii. 482-488.
- Sheldon, 287.
- Thomas, 216.
- Von Holst, i. 470.
- Wilson, Epochs Am. History, 43, 44.
- Winsor, vii. 254.

Two Indian Wars

Black Hawk, 1832.

Osceola and the Seminoles, 1835.

- Bryant & Gay, iv. 295, 350-354.
- Coffin, Building the Nation, 301, 302.
- Higginson, 263, 264.
- Johnston, 223, 224.
- Lalor, Cyclopædia, iii. 732.
- Montgomery, 244, Note, 245.
- Nicolay & Hay, Life of Lincoln, i. 87-100.
- Patton, ii. 727, 728.
- Richardson, 363, 364.
- Sargent, Public Men and Events, i. 246, 247, 319.
- Schouler, iv. 319, 320.
- Sheldon, 254, 287.
- Thomas, 208, 209.
- Von Holst, ii. 298–310.
- Wilson, Rise and fall of Slave Power, i. 512, 527.
- Winsor, vii. 406, 407.

Removals from Office

"To the victors belong the spoils."
Daniel Marcy.

"To give to every change of parties, as the national patronage grows, the character of a revolution is to imperil the safety of our institutions at a vital point, and put up the Republic at sale."

"If you git me inside the White House, Your head with ile I'll kinder 'nint, By gittin you inside the lighthouse, Down to the end of Jaalem Pint."
Lowell.

- Adams, Hist. U.S., i. 223-229.
- Benton, Thirty Years' View, chap. 50.
- Bryant & Gay, iv. 297, 298.
- Bryce, Am. Commonwealth, ii. 125-132.
- Eggleston, 266.
- Fiske, Hist. of U.S., 308, 309.
- Higginson, 265.
- Irving-Fiske, 543, 544.
- Johnston, 225, 226.
- Lalor, Cyclopædia, iii. 565-569.
- Montgomery, 236, 237.
- Patton, ii. 704.
- Sargent, Public Men and Events, i. 164, 165.
- Schouler, iii. 453-462.
- Smith, Goldwin, 196.
- Sumner, Life of Jackson, 146-148.
- Thomas, 202, 203.
- Von Holst, ii. 23-27.
- Wilson, Epochs Am. History, 30-35.

Period of Critical Change

Nullification and Calhoun

" In case of a plain, palpable violation of the Constitution, a State may interpose, and arrest, or nullify, the law within her own borders for her own protection."
Calhoun.

- Benton, Thirty Years' View, 140-172.
- Bryant & Gay, iv. 306-309.
- Coffin, Building the Nation. 248-250.
- Eggleston, 267, 269, 304.
- Fiske, Hist. of U.S., 309-311.
- Greeley, American Conflict, i. 93-100.
- Higginson, 262, 263.
- Irving-Fiske, 542.
- Johnston, Hist. of Am. Politics, 112, 113.
- Johnston, 229, 230.
- Lalor, Cyclopædia, ii. 1050-1055.
- Montgomery, 240-243.
- Patton, ii. 707-709, 718, 719.
- Rhodes, i. 40-50.
- Richardson, 360-363.
- Sargent, i. 175-177.
- Schouler, iv. 38-41, 97-102.
- Schurz, Life of Clay, ii. 2-10.
- Sheldon, 238-240.
- Smith, Goldwin, 201.
- Sumner, Life of Jackson, 207-212, 217-221.
- Thomas, 205, 206.
- Von Holst, i. 465-492.
- Wilson, Epochs Am. History, 47, 56-62.
- Winsor, vii. 253, 254, 322.

The President's Hostility to the National Bank

- Benton, i. 158, 159.
- Bryant & Gay, iv. 300-302.
- Fiske, Hist. of U.S., 307, 312, 313.
- Irving-Fiske, 544, 545.
- Johnston, 226.
- Lalor, Cyclopædia, i. 209.
- Montgomery, 239, 240.
- Patton, ii. 707.
- Richardson, 357.
- Sargent, Public Men and Events, i. 213-215, 219-224.
- Schouler, iv. 44-54.
- Schurz, Life of Clay, i. 62-66.
- Smith, Goldwin, 198, 199.

The President's Hostility to the National Bank
(*Continued*)

- Sumner, Life of Jackson, 233-250.
- Thomas, 205.
- Von Holst, ii. 31, 32, 37-45.
- Wilson, Epochs Am. History, 69-74, 79, 80.
- Winsor, vii. 283, 284.

The Compromise Tariff of 1833

Henry Clay its Author.

- Benton, Thirty Years' View, i. 313-330.
- Bryant & Gay, iv. 305.
- Fiske, Hist. of U.S., 312.
- Irving-Fiske, 542.
- Johnston, 231.
- Lalor, Cyclopædia, iii. 862, 863.
- Patton, ii. 725, 726.
- Sargent, Public Men and Events, i. 189-192.
- Schouler, iv. 102-106.
- Schurz, Life of Clay, i. 357-365.
- Sheldon, 267.
- Smith, Goldwin, 201.
- Sumner, Life of Jackson, 285-291.
- Taussig, Tariff Hist. of the U.S., 109-111.
- Thomas, 207.
- Von Holst, i. 491, 492, 497-499; ii., 177.
- Wilson, Epochs of Am. History, 65-68.
- Winsor, vii. 286, 287.

The first asylum for the blind in the United States opened, 1832.

Second Administration of Andrew Jackson 1833-1837

Removal of the Government Funds from the U.S. Bank

- Benton, i. 373-379.
- Bryant & Gay, iv. 301, 302.
- Fiske, Hist. of U.S., 312.
- Higginson, Larger Hist. U.S., 452.
- Irving-Fiske, 545.
- Johnston, 226.
- Lalor, Cyclopædia, i. 203, 209, 798, 799.
- Montgomery, 239, 240.
- Patton, ii. 726, 727.
- Richardson, 357, 358.
- Sargent, Public Men and Events, 258-261, 276.

Period of Critical Change

Removal of the Government Funds from the U.S. Bank *(Continued)*
- Schouler, iv. 132-144.
- Schurz, Life of Clay, ii. 25-51.
- Smith, Goldwin, 199.
- Sumner, Life of Jackson, 296-321.
- Thomas, 206.
- Von Holst, ii. 51-66.
- Wilson, Epochs Am. History, 80-82.
- Winsor, vii. 285.

Introduction of the Locomotive and the Railway System
- Bryant, iv. 313, 314.
- Coffin, Building the Nation, 302, 428-431.
- Eggleston, 273-274.
- Fiske, Hist. of U.S., 314-316.
- Higginson, 260.
- Irving-Fiske, 542.
- Johnston, 215, 216.
- Lalor, Cyclopædia, iii. 494.
- Montgomery, 231-233.
- Richardson, 354-357.
- Schouler, iv. 125-131.
- Sheldon, 251, 285.
- Smith, Goldwin, 218.
- Thomas, 209-213.
- Wilson, Epochs Am. History, 102, 103.

The first railway in the United States at Quincy, Mass., 1826.
The first locomotive imported from England by the Delaware and Hudson Canal Company, 1828.

The Anti-Slavery Movement Organization of the Am. Anti-Slavery Society Garrison and the Liberator

"I will not equivocate, I will not excuse, I will not retreat a

- Blaine, i. 21-25.
- Bryant & Gay, iv. 316-318, 324-328.
- Coffin, Building the Nation, 285-287.
- Fiske, Hist. of U.S., 322, 323.
- Garrison. Life of Garrison, i. 219-276.
- Greeley, Am. Conflict, i. 115-121, 130-142.
- Higginson, 264-265.
- Irving-Fiske, 543.
- Johnston, 223.
- Lalor, Cyclopædia, i. 4, 5.
- Montgomery, 237-238.
- Patton, ii. 863, 864.

The Anti-Slavery Movement

Organization of the Am. Anti-Slavery Society

Garrison and the Liberator

(Continued)

single inch, and I will be heard."
William Lloyd Garrison.

- Richardson, 413-417.
- Rhodes, i. 53-54, 58-75.
- Sargent, Public Men and Events, i. 294, 295.
- Schouler, iv. 210-214, 219-229.
- Sheldon, 243, 286.
- Smith, Goldwin, 229-233.
- Thomas, 217.
- Von Holst, ii. 80-125.
- Wilson, Epochs Am. History, 121-123.
- Wilson, Rise and Fall of Slave Power, i. 176-185, 223-230, 248-263.
- Winsor, vii. 287, 288.

Rise of American Literature

Longfellow, Whittier, Hawthorne, Holmes, Bancroft, Prescott, all began to be noted during the decade 1830-1840.

- Eggleston, 378-380.
- Fiske, Hist. of U.S., 325.
- Irving-Fiske, 543.
- Johnston, 222.
- Montgomery, 245, 246.
- Patton, ii. 1155.
- Schouler, iv. 354-356.
- Sheldon, 286.
- Thomas, 215, 216.
- Wilson, Epochs Am. History, 108-111.

Independence of Texas

- Benton, Thirty Years' View, i. 655-660.
- Blaine, i. 26.
- Bryant & Gay, iv. 361-363.
- Coffin, Building the Nation, 291-300.
- Fiske, Hist. of U.S., 325.
- Greeley, Am. Conflict, i. 147.
- Irving-Fiske, 547.
- Johnston, 241, 242.
- Lalor, Cyclopædia, iii. 921.
- McMaster, iv.
- Montgomery, 255, 256.
- Patton, ii. 742-748.
- Richardson, 372-374.
- Rhodes, i. 75, 76.
- Sargent, Public Men and Events, i. 316-318; ii. 62, 63.

Period of Critical Change

Independence of Texas
(Continued)

- Schouler, iv. 247-254.
- Sumner, Life of Jackson, 352-357.
- Thomas, 232.
- Von Holst, ii. 548-571.
- Williams, Life of Sam Houston, 53-73, 184-217.
- Wilson, Epochs Am. History, 141, 142.
- Wilson, Rise and Fall of Slave Power, i. 587-590.
- Winsor, vii. 505, 551.

Arkansas admitted, 1836. The twenty-fifth State.
Michigan admitted, 1837. The twenty-sixth State.

French Spoliation Claims

A contest for the recognition of the rights of citizens of the United States.
France pays an indemnity of twenty-five million francs.

- Benton, Thirty Years' View, i. 588-600.
- Johnston, 224.
- Lalor, Cyclopædia, iii. 946, 947.
- McMaster, iv.
- Schouler, iv. 184, 239-244.
- Sumner, Life of Jackson, 170, 171.
- Thomas, 157.
- Wilson, Epochs Am. History, 86.
- Winsor, vii. 496, 497.

The McCormick Reaper patented, 1834.

Election of the Eighth President Martin Van Buren

Richard M. Johnson chosen Vice-President by vote of the Senate.
The only occurrence of such a choice in U.S. history.
See twelfth Article of Amendments.

- Coffin, Building the Nation, 302.
- Eggleston, 269.
- Fiske, Hist. of U.S., 314.
- Irving-Fiske, 545.
- Johnston, Hist. Am. Politics, 123-125.
- Johnston, 231-233.
- Lalor, Cyclopædia, iii. 1061.
- McMaster, iv.
- Montgomery, 246.
- Patton, ii. 730.
- Richardson, 364, 367.
- Sargent, Public Men and Events, ii. 10.
- Schouler, iv. 274-276.
- Sheldon, 287.
- Shepard, Life of Van Buren, 238-241.

Election of the Eighth President Martin Van Buren (*Continued*)
- Smith, Goldwin, 205, 206.
- Stanwood, Presidential Elections, 111-122.
- Thomas, 219, 220.
- Von Holst, ii. 147-159.
- Wilson, Epochs of Am. History, 91, 92.
- Winsor, vii. 288, 289.

Administration of Martin Van Buren 1837-1841

The Panic of 1837
- Benton, Thirty Years' View, ii. 9-12.
- Bryant & Gay, iv. 312.
- Coffin, Building the Nation, 302, 303.
- Eggleston, 276.
- Fiske, Hist. of U.S., 317, 318.
- Irving-Fiske, 545.
- Johnston, Hist. Am. Politics, 126.
- Johnston, 234.
- Lalor, Cyclopædia, ii. 192.
- McMaster, iv.
- Montgomery, 247, 248.
- Patton, ii. 731-734.
- Richardson, 367.
- Sargent, Public Men and Events, ii. 10-15.
- Schouler, iv. 276-281.
- Shepard, Life of Van Buren, 242-277.
- Smith, Goldwin, 206.
- Thomas, 220, 221.
- Von Holst, ii. 177, 178, 195-200.
- Wilson, Epochs Am. History, 93.
- Winsor, vii. 289.

The Independent or Sub-Treasury
- Benton, Thirty Years' View, ii. 124, 125.
- Bryant, iv. 312.
- Fiske, Hist. of U.S., 318.
- Irving-Fiske, 545.
- Johnston, Hist. Am. Politics, 126-129.
- Johnston, 235.
- Lalor, Cyclopædia, ii. 493-496.
- McMaster, iv.
- Montgomery, 248, 249.

Period of Critical Change 55

The Independent or Sub-Treasury
(*Continued*)
- Patton, ii. 733.
- Sargent, Public Men and Events, ii. 32-51.
- Schouler, iv. 283-285, 324-326.
- Schurz, Life of Clay, ii. 136-144.
- Shepard, Life of Van Buren, 282, 289, 295-297.
- Thomas, 222, 223.
- Von Holst, Life of Calhoun, 184-187.
- Von Holst, ii. 201-203, 211, 216-218.
- Wilson, Epochs Am. History, 97, 98.
- Winsor, vii. 289.

The Caroline Affair
- Benton, Thirty Years' View, ii. 276-291.
- Bryant & Gay, iv. 355, 356.
- Johnston, 237.
- Lalor, Cyclopædia, ii. 822.
- Lodge, Life of Webster, 247-249.
- McMaster, iv.
- Montgomery, 248, Note.
- Patton, ii. 738, 739.
- Sargent, Public Men and Events, ii. 30-32.
- Schouler, iv. 396-398.
- Shepard, Life of Van Buren, 300-305.
- Schurz, Life of Clay, ii. 150.
- Thomas, 223.
- Winsor, vii. 494.

Friction matches begin to be used, 1838.
Charles Goodyear, of Connecticut, discovers the process of vulcanizing India rubber, 1839.

Slavery Riots and the Right of Petition

See First Amendment to the Constitution.
- Blaine, i. 21-25.
- Bryant & Gay, iv. 330-339.
- Coffin, Building the Nation, 308-313.
- Fiske, Hist. of U.S., 323.
- Greeley, Am. Conflict, i. 126, 127, 130-142, 145-147.
- Higginson, 268.
- Johnston, 236, 237.
- Lalor, Cyclopædia, iii. 167-169.
- Montgomery, 238, 239.

Slavery Riots and the Right of Petition
(Continued)

"Let it be once understood, that the sacred right of petition and the cause of the abolitionists must rise or fall together, and the consequences may be fatal."
James Buchanan.

Morse, Life of John Q. Adams, 243-275.
Rhodes, i. 60, 61, 69-72.
Richardson, 414, 415.
Sargent, Public Men and Events, ii. 51-55, 59-61.
Schouler, iv. 299, 300, 307, 308, 423, 424.
Sheldon, 287.
Thomas, 223, 224.
Von Holst, ii. 221, 222, 236-240, 245, 247, 272.
Wilson, Epochs Am. History, 114, 122.
Wilson, Rise and Fall of Slave Power, i. 374-389, 394-399, 424-438.
Winsor, vii. 287, 288.

Election of the Ninth and Tenth Presidents Wm. Henry Harrison and John Tyler as Vice-President

Victory of the Whigs; Democrats yield the power they have held for forty years.

"No Vice-President of the U.S. ever was or ever will be voted for under the expectation that he will be anything more than Vice-President."

Bryant & Gay, iv. 356, 357, 359.
Coffin, Building the Nation, 304.
Eggleston, 276, 277.
Fiske, Hist. of U.S., 319.
Greeley, Am. Conflict, i. 154.
Higginson, 269, 270.
Irving-Fiske, 545.
Johnston, Hist. Am. Politics, 130-132.
Johnston, 238, 239.
Lalor, Cyclopædia, ii. 57; iii. 1104, 1105.
Montgomery, 251, 252.
Patton, ii. 734.
Rhodes, i. 78.
Richardson, 368, 369.
Sargent, Public Men and Events, ii. 93-96, 105, 106, 107-111, 120-122.
Schouler, iv. 335-341, 359-366.
Sheldon, 288.
Smith, Goldwin, 207-209.
Stanwood, Presidential Elections, 123-140.
Thomas, 224, 225.
Wilson, Epochs Am. History, 133, 134.
Wilson, Rise and Fall of Slave Power, i. 421.
Winsor, vii. 289, 290.

Summary of the Period of Critical Change 1829-1842

1829
- Inauguration of Andrew Jackson.
- The Kitchen Cabinet.

1830
- Removals from Office.
- Webster-Hayne Debate.

1832
- The Black Hawk War.
- Nullification and Calhoun.
- First Asylum for the Blind.

1833
- American Anti-Slavery Society Organized.
- The Compromise Tariff.
- Beginning of Jackson's Second Term.
- The President's Hostility to the National Bank.
- Removal of the Government Funds from the United States Bank.
- First American Locomotive.

1834
- McCormick's Reaping-Machine.

1835
- Osceola and the Seminoles.

1836
- Election of Martin Van Buren.
- Arkansas Admitted.

1837
- Michigan Admitted.
- Inauguration of Martin Van Buren.
- Independence of Texas.
- Rise of American Literature.
- French Spoliation Claims.
- The Panic of 1837.
- The Independent or Sub-Treasury.
- The Caroline Affair.

1838
- Slavery Riots and the Right of Petition.

1840
- Election of Wm. Henry Harrison and John Tyler.

1841
- Inauguration of President Harrison.
- Death of Harrison and Succession of Tyler.

Period of Slavery Agitation 1842–1856

Administrations of Wm. Henry Harrison and John Tyler 1841-1845

Tariff of 1842

A return to moderate protective duties.

- Benton, Thirty Years' View, ii. 417.
- Blaine, i. 192-195.
- Johnston, Hist. Am. Politics, 135, 136.
- Johnston, 240.
- Lalor, Cyclopædia, iii. 863.
- Sargent, Public Men and Events, ii. 171, 176, 177, 184-188.
- Schouler, iv. 406-410.
- Sheldon, 288.
- Taussig, Tariff History of U.S., 112-114.
- Von Holst, ii. 451-454, 463.
- Wilson, Epochs Am. History, 140.
- Winsor, vii. 290, 355.

Annexation of Texas

"Annexation meant sectional, and not national advantage in this age."
Schouler.

- Benton, ii. 581, 599-619.
- Blaine, i. 28-40.
- Bryant & Gay, iv. 362-364, 367-369.
- Draper, Hist. of Civil War, i. 394, 443.
- Eggleston, 278.
- Fiske, Hist. of U.S., 325-327.
- Greeley, Am. Conflict, i. 156-174.
- Higginson, 271, 272.
- Irving-Fiske, 547, 548.
- Johnston, 242.
- Lalor, Cyclopædia, i. 96, 97; iii. 921.
- Montgomery, 255, 256.
- Patton, ii. 747-749.
- Rhodes, i. 76-86.
- Richardson, 373-375.
- Sargent, Public Men and Events, ii. 201, 222, 259-263.
- Schouler, iv. 440-442, 449-459.

Period of Slavery Agitation

Annexation of Texas
(Continued)

Smith, Goldwin, 209, 210.
Thomas, 233.
Von Holst, ii. 612-614, 625-628, 634-640, 643, 644, 657-680, 709-712.
Williams, Life of Sam Houston, 289-295.
Wilson, Epochs Am. History, 141-147.
Wilson, Rise and Fall of Slave Power, i. 587-620.
Winsor, vii. 291, 506.

Administration of John Tyler 1841-1845

The Webster-Ashburton Treaty

Settled the question of the north boundary as far west as the Rocky Mountains. The U.S. gained seven-twelfths of the territory in dispute in northern Maine.

"Contained the only agreement, since the Treaty of Jay, made with any power for the surrender of persons charged with the commission of crimes."
J. C. Bancroft Davis.

See Art. "Extradition," Lalor, Cyclopædia, Vol. ii.

Benton, ii. 420-452.
Blaine, i. 26, 49.
Bryant & Gay, iv. 365, 366.
Fiske, Hist. of U.S., 321.
Haswell, Treaties and Conventions, 432-438.
Higginson, 270.
Johnston, 241.
Lalor, Cyclopædia, iii. 947.
Lodge, Life of Webster, 252-260.
Montgomery, 253.
Patton, ii. 740-742.
Rhodes, i. 78.
Sargent, Public Men and Events, ii. 163, 164.
Schouler, iv. 398-404.
Sheldon, 288.
Thomas, 226, 227.
Wilson, Epochs Am. History, 140, 141.
Winsor, vii. 179, 292, 493, 525, 554.

Dorr's Rebellion

"Of all the United States, Rhode Island, the last and most reluctant of the old thirteen to enter the

Bryant and Gay, iv. 366, 367.
Fiske, Hist. of U.S., 320.
Higginson, 270.
Johnston, 244, 245.
Lalor, Cyclopædia, i. 835.
Montgomery, 253.

Dorr's Rebellion
(Continued)

Union, was the latest to preserve a royal charter as the basis of fundamental law."

- Patton, ii. 749, 750.
- Schouler, iv. 462, 463.
- Thomas, 227, 228.
- Wilson, Epochs Am. History, 161.
- Winsor, vii. 355.

The Mormons

- Bryant & Gay, iv. 427, 428.
- Coffin, Building the Nation, 440-449.
- Eggleston, 367.
- Fiske, Hist. of U.S., 321.
- Higginson, 270.
- Johnston, 237.
- Lalor, Cyclopædia, ii. 910-912.
- Montgomery, 249, 250.
- Patton, ii. 837-839.
- Schouler, iv. 312, 546-549.
- Sheldon, 288.
- Thomas, 230, 231.

The First Electric Telegraph
Samuel F. B. Morse

"What hath God wrought?"

- Benton, Thirty Years' View, ii. 578.
- Bryant & Gay, iv. 315.
- Coffin, Building the Nation, 433, 434.
- Eggleston, 274.
- Fiske, Hist. of U.S., 326.
- Higginson, 273.
- Johnston, 243, 244.
- Lalor, Cyclopædia, iii. 890, 891.
- Montgomery, 254, 255.
- Patton, ii. 1032.
- Richardson, 369-371.
- Sargent, Public Men and Events, ii. 192-194, 231-232.
- Schouler, iv. 469, 470.
- Sheldon, 252, 253.
- Thomas, 229, 230.
- Wilson, Epochs Am. History, 162.

Florida admitted, 1845.
Ether first used as an anæsthetic by Dr. Charles T. Jackson, of Boston, about 1840.

Period of Slavery Agitation 61

**Election of the Eleventh President
James K. Polk
George M. Dallas
Vice-President**

The most closely contested election to this period of U.S. History, except that of 1800.
The first "dark horse."
The question of Texas Annexation was practically the question of the Campaign.

{
Bryant & Gay, iv. 368.
Eggleston, 277, 278.
Fiske, Hist. of U.S., 326.
Greeley, Am. Conflict, i. 164-168.
Higginson, 273.
Irving-Fiske, 547, 548.
Johnston, Hist. Am. Politics, 138, 139.
Johnston, 245, 246.
Lalor, Cyclopædia, ii. 57; i'i. 278.
Montgomery, 256.
Patton, ii. 751.
Rhodes, i. 82, 83.
Richardson, 375.
Sargent, Public Men and Events, ii. 232-269.
Schouler, iv. 471-480, 495-500.
Sheldon, 288.
Smith, Goldwin, 210, 211.
Stanwood, Presidential Elections, 140-160.
Thomas, 234.
Von Holst, ii. 694-701.
Wilson, Epochs Am. History, 145-147.
Wilson, Rise and Fall of Slave Power, i. 603-605.
Winsor, vii. 291.
}

Administration of James K. Polk 1845-1849

The Oregon Boundary Dispute

"Fifty-four-Forty, or Fight," though the Forty-ninth parallel was afterward acceded to.

For full text of treaty, see Haswell, "Treaties and Conventions," 438, 439.

{
Blaine, i. 48-56.
Bryant and Gay, iv. 366.
Coffin, Building the Nation, 363-386.
Eggleston, 286, 287.
Fiske, Hist. of U.S., 321, 322.
Haswell, Treaties and Conventions, 438, 439.
Irving-Fiske, 546.
Johnston, Hist. Am. Politics, 144.
Johnston, 250, 251.
Lalor, Cyclopædia, ii. 1045-1047.
Montgomery, 256-258.
}

Handbook of American History

The Oregon Boundary Dispute
(Continued)

- Patton, ii. 753-756.
- Rhodes, i. 86.
- Richardson, 396.
- Sargent, Public Men and Events, ii. 269-282.
- Schouler, iv. 504-514.
- Sheldon, 256-260.
- Smith, Goldwin, 174.
- Thomas, 242-244.
- Von Holst, iii. 29-60.
- Wilson, Epochs Am. History, 147, 148.
- Winsor, vii. 510, 511, 559-562.

Texas admitted, 1845.
Elias Howe, of Massachusetts, first receives a patent for the sewing-machine, 1846.

The Texan Boundary Dispute

- Blaine, i, 62-64.
- Bryant & Gay, iv. 369.
- Coffin, Building the Nation, 314, 317.
- Eggleston, 279.
- Fiske, Hist. of U.S., 326, 327.
- Greeley, Am. Conflict, i. 186, 187.
- Higginson, 274.
- Irving-Fiske, 548.
- Jay, Hist. Mexican War, 147-150.
- Johnston, 251.
- Lalor, Cyclopædia, iii. 921.
- Montgomery, 259.
- Patton, ii. 752, 753.
- Rhodes, i. 87, 88.
- Richardson, 373-376.
- Sargent, ii. 270, 291.
- Schouler, iv. 523-526.
- Sheldon, 268.
- Thomas, 237.
- Von Holst, iii. 83-92.
- Wilson, Epochs Am. History, 149, 150.
- Wilson, Rise and Fall of Slave Power, ii. 7-17.
- Winsor, vii. 408, 440-443.

Period of Slavery Agitation 63

Iowa admitted, 1846.

The Mexican War in General

"Of the volunteers who enrolled for this war, nearly two-thirds came from south of Mason and Dixon's line; but accident and opportunity gave the chief military renown of the war to the Whigs."
Schouler.

- Blaine, i. 62-65.
- Bryant & Gay, iv. 369.
- Coffin, Building the Nation, 314-318.
- Comte de Paris, Hist. of the Civil War, i. 30-58.
- Draper, Hist. of Civil War, i. 395-399.
- Eggleston, 279, 286.
- Fiske, Hist. of U.S., 327.
- Greeley, Am. Conflict, i. 186, 187.
- Higginson, 274.
- Johnston, 251.
- Lalor, Cyclopædia, iii. 1090, 1091.
- Montgomery, 259.
- Patton, ii. 751-753.
- Rhodes, i. 87, 88, 92, 93.
- Richardson, 375, 376.
- Sargent, Public Men and Events, ii. 291-301.
- Schouler, iv. 521-526, 535-538.
- Sheldon, 268.
- Smith, Goldwin, 211, 212.
- Thomas, 237, 238.
- Von Holst, iii. 207-215, 230-237.
- Wilson, Epochs Am. History, 149-152.
- Wilson, Rise and Fall of Slave Power, ii. 7-13.
- Winsor, vii. 408, 409.

The War in Detail

Taylor's Campaign in the North

Whittier's "Angels of Buena Vista."

- Bryant & Gay, iv. 369-372, 374, 375.
- Coffin, Building the Nation, 318-331.
- Eggleston, 279, 280.
- Fiske, Hist. of U.S., 327.
- Greeley, Am. Conflict, i. 187.
- Higginson, 274, 275.
- Johnston, 251, 252, 254, 255.
- Lalor, Cyclopædia, iii. 1091.
- Montgomery, 259, 260.
- Patton, ii. 756-789.

The War in Detail

Taylor's Campaign in the North *(Continued)*
- Richardson, 376-380, 387, 388.
- Sargent, Public Men and Events, ii. 301-304, 325, 326.
- Sheldon, 272.
- Schouler, v. 14-38.
- Thomas, 238.
- Von Holst, iii. 234-238, 256, 330, 331.
- Wilson, Epochs Am. History, 150, 151.
- Winsor, vii. 408, 409.

Fremont's Campaign in California
- Bryant & Gay, iv. 373.
- Coffin, Building the Nation, 355-358.
- Eggleston, 283, 284.
- Fiske, Hist. of U.S., 327.
- Higginson, 277.
- Johnston, 253.
- Lalor, Cyclopædia, i. 98.
- Montgomery, 260.
- Patton, ii. 793-796.
- Richardson, 385, 386.
- Royce, Hist. of California, 48-150.
- Sargent, Public Men and Events, ii. 298, 299.
- Sheldon, 270, 271.
- Schouler, iv. 530-535.
- Thomas, 240.
- Von Holst, iii. 224-230.
- Wilson, Epochs Am. History, 152.
- Winsor, vii. 410, 445.

Kearney's Campaign in New Mexico
- Bryant & Gay, iv. 372.
- Coffin, Building the Nation, 349.
- Eggleston, 283.
- Higginson, 277.
- Johnston, 253.
- Lalor, Cyclopædia, i. 98.
- Patton, ii. 796-798.
- Richardson, 380-385.
- Sargent, Public Men and Events, ii. 298.
- Schouler, iv. 528.

Period of Slavery Agitation 65

Kearney's Campaign in New Mexico
(*Continued*)

- Sheldon, 268, 269.
- Thomas, 238, 239.
- Von Holst, iii. 258-262.
- Wilson, Epochs Am. History, 152.
- Winsor, vii. 409, 410.

Scott's Campaign in Central Mexico

- Bryant & Gay, iv. 376-385.
- Coffin, Building the Nation, 332-350.
- Eggleston, 284, 285.
- Fiske, Hist. of U.S., 327, 328.
- Higginson, 275-277.
- Irving-Fiske, 549.
- Johnston, 256-259.
- Lalor, Cyclopædia, iii. 1092.
- Patton, ii. 804-822.
- Richardson, 389-396.
- Sargent, Public Men and Events, ii. 326-330.
- Sheldon, 273-275.
- Schouler, v. 42-61.
- Thomas, 240.
- Von Holst, iii. 331-333.
- Wilson, Epochs Am. History, 151, 152.
- Winsor, vii. 411, 412.

The Wilmot Proviso

"What shall be done with newly acquired territory? is the question that opens this the second volume of the history of the Union under the Constitution."

- Blaine, i. 66-68.
- Bryant & Gay, iv. 385, 386.
- Coffin, Building the Nation, 391, 392.
- Draper, Hist. of Civil War, i. 400.
- Eggleston, 293.
- Fiske, Hist. of U.S., 328.
- Greeley, Am. Conflict, 189.
- Higginson, 279.
- Irving-Fiske, 549, 550.
- Johnston, 260.
- Lalor, Cyclopædia, iii. 1114.
- Montgomery, 262, Note v.
- Nicolay & Hay, Life of Lincoln, i. 268.
- Patton, ii. 827.
- Rhodes, i. 90.

The Wilmot Proviso
(Continued)

- Sargent, Public Men and Events, ii. 309, 310.
- Schouler, iv. 543, 544.
- Schurz, Life of Clay, ii. 285.
- Smith, Goldwin, 213.
- Thomas, 246.
- Von Holst, iii. 305-308.
- Wilson, Epochs Am. History, 152-154.
- Wilson, Rise and Fall of Slave Power, ii. 16, 17, 24.
- Winsor, vii. 292, 293.

Treaty of Guadalupe Hidalgo July 4, 1848 The $15,000,000 Indemnity

For full text of Treaty, see Haswell's Treaties and Conventions, 681-692.

- Bryant & Gay, iv. 387.
- Coffin, Building the Nation, 350.
- Eggleston, 286.
- Fiske, Hist. of U.S., 328.
- Haswell, Treaties and Conventions, 681-692.
- Higginson, 277.
- Irving-Fiske, 549.
- Johnston, 259.
- Lalor, Cyclopædia, i. 98; iii. 947.
- Patton, ii. 823.
- Rhodes, i. 92, 93.
- Richardson, 396.
- Sargent, Public Men and Events, ii. 329.
- Sheldon, 275.
- Schouler, v. 84, 87, 88.
- Schurz, Life of Clay, ii. 300.
- Thomas, 241, 242.
- Von Holst, iii. 344, 345.
- Wilson, Epochs Am. History, 152, 153.
- Wilson, Rise and Fall of Slave Power, ii. 25.
- Winsor, vii. 506, 553.

Tariff of 1846

Protection entirely excluded from this act.

- Blaine, i. 195.
- Johnston, 249.
- Lalor, Cyclopædia, iii. 865.
- Patton, ii. 827.

Period of Slavery Agitation

Tariff of 1846
(Continued)

- Sargent, Public Men and Events, ii. 285, 286.
- Schouler, iv. 515-517.
- Taussig, History of U.S. Tariffs, 114, 156.
- Thomas, 244.
- Von Holst, iii. 278-280.
- Wilson, Epochs Am. History, 154.
- Winsor, vii. 293.

The Discovery of Gold, 1848 and the Emigration to California

"That splendid and startling discovery was made in fact before the actual conclusion of a treaty with Mexico." *Schouler.*

- Blaine, i. 88.
- Bryant & Gay, iv. 387, 388.
- Coffin, Building the Nation, 359-362.
- Eggleston, 284, 294.
- Fiske, Hist. of U.S., 328, 329.
- Higginson, 278.
- Irving-Fiske, 550.
- Johnston, 261, 262.
- Lalor, Cyclopædia, i. 329, 330.
- Montgomery, 263-265.
- Patton, ii. 825, 826.
- Rhodes, i. 111.
- Richardson, 398, 401.
- Royce, Hist. of California, 220-246.
- Schouler, v. 133-141.
- Sheldon, 276, 278.
- Thomas, 244, 245.
- Von Holst, iii. 404-407.
- Wilson, Epochs Am. History, 162.

Wisconsin admitted, 1848.

The Buffalo Convention and the Anti-Slavery Revolt

Formation of the Free-Soil Party.

- Blaine, i. 81, 82.
- Bryant & Gay, iv. 386.
- Eggleston, 293.
- Fiske, Hist. of U.S., 330.
- Greeley, Am. Conflict, i. 191, 192.
- Higginson, 279, 280.
- Irving-Fiske, 550.
- Johnston, 261.
- Lalor, Cyclopædia, ii. 287, 288.

The Buffalo Convention and the Anti-Slavery Revolt
(*Continued*)

- Patton, ii. 827, 828.
- Rhodes, i. 97.
- Sargent, Public Men and Events, ii. 335.
- Schouler, v. 103-106.
- Schurz, Life of Clay, ii. 309-314.
- Smith, Goldwin, 214.
- Thomas, 247.
- Von Holst, iii. 397-400.
- Wilson, Epochs Am. History, 158, 159.
- Wilson, Rise and Fall of Slave Power, ii. 150-160.
- Winsor, vii. 293.

Election of the Twelfth and Thirteenth Presidents Zachary Taylor and Millard Fillmore

- Blaine, i. 81-83.
- Bryant & Gay, iv. 386.
- Coffin, Building the Nation, 392, 393.
- Eggleston, 293.
- Fiske, Hist. of U.S., 329, 330.
- Greeley, Am. Conflict, i. 191-193.
- Higginson, 280.
- Irving-Fiske, 550.
- Johnston, Hist. Am. Politics, 147, 148.
- Johnston, 261.
- Lalor, Cyclopædia, ii. 58.
- Montgomery, 265.
- Patton, ii. 827-829.
- Rhodes, i. 97.
- Richardson, 397.
- Schouler, v. 100-114.
- Sheldon, 289.
- Smith, Goldwin, 212, 213.
- Stanwood, Presidential Elections, 161-177.
- Thomas, 246, 247.
- Von Holst, iii. 402, 403.
- Wilson, Epochs Am. History, 157, 158.
- Wilson, Rise and Fall of Slave Power, ii. 129-139.
- Winsor, vii. 293.

Period of Slavery Agitation 69

Administration of Zachary Taylor 1849-1850

The Compromise of 1850 or the "Omnibus Bill"

Not adopted as a whole, yet all its provisions were adopted separately.

- Benton, Thirty Years' View, ii. 742.
- Blaine, i. 91, 94, 95, 96, 97.
- Bryant & Gay, iv. 391-394.
- Bryce, Am. Commonwealths, ii. 12, 13.
- Coffin, Building the Nation, 387-398.
- Eggleston, 295.
- Fiske, Hist. of U.S., 337, 338.
- Greeley, Am. Conflict, i. 203-208.
- Higginson, 280.
- Irving-Fiske, 551.
- Johnston, 266.
- Lalor, Cyclopædia, i. 552, 553.
- Lodge, Life of Webster, 300.
- Montgomery, 266, 267.
- Morse, Life of Lincoln, i. 89-93.
- Nicolay & Hay, Life of Lincoln, i. 326-329.
- Patton, ii. 834, 835, 837.
- Rhodes, i. 122-135, 172, 173, 181-183.
- Richardson, 409.
- Sargent, Public Men and Events, ii. 357, 369.
- Schouler, v. 162-166, 178-182, 198-201.
- Schurz, Life of Clay, ii. 315-372.
- Sheldon, 292.
- Smith, Goldwin, 213, 214.
- Thomas, 249.
- Von Holst, iii. 484, 485, 523-526.
- Wilson, Epochs Am. History, 169-174.
- Wilson, Rise and Fall of Slave Power, ii. 233-241, 273, 282, 283.
- Winsor, vii. 255.

California admitted, 1850.

Webster's Seventh of March Speech

- Blaine, i. 92-94.
- Bryant & Gay, iv. 392, 393.
- Coffin, Building the Nation, 395.

Webster's Seventh of March Speech (*Continued*)

See Whittier's *Ichabod*.

"Great wrong has been done him in attributing it solely to the conscious object of getting himself installed in the White House."
Von Holst.

- Greeley, Am. Conflict, i. 205, 206.
- Lalor, Cyclopædia, iii. 1098.
- Lodge, Life of Webster, 301-332.
- Montgomery, 267.
- Rhodes, i. 142-158.
- Sargent, Public Men and Events, ii. 362.
- Schouler, v. 167-170.
- Sheldon, 294.
- Thomas, 249, 250.
- Von Holst, iii. 497-507.
- Wilson, Epochs Am. History, 170.
- Wilson, Rise and Fall of Slave Power, ii. 242-246.

The Fugitive Slave Law

- Benton, Thirty Years' View, ii. 773-780.
- Blaine, i. 96.
- Bryant & Gay, iv. 395, 396.
- Coffin, Building the Nation, 394, 399-406.
- Eggleston, 294, 295.
- Greeley, Am. Conflict, i. 210-219.
- Higginson, 281.
- Irving-Fiske, 551.
- Johnston, 267.
- Lalor, Cyclopædia, ii. 316, 317.
- Montgomery, 268.
- Patton, ii. 837.
- Rhodes, i. 185-189.
- Richardson, 417-420.
- Schouler, v. 199, 204-208.
- Schurz, Life of Clay, ii. 369-372.
- Sheldon, 291-298.
- Smith, Goldwin, 214.
- Thomas, 249, 250.
- Von Holst, iv. 15-22.
- Wilson, Epochs Am. History, 174-178.
- Wilson, Rise and Fall of Slave Power, ii. 352-359.

Administration of Millard Fillmore 1850-1853

An International Question
Correspondence of Webster and Hülsemann.
- Lodge, Life of Webster, 333-336.
- Rhodes, i. 205, 206.
- Schouler, v. 236, 237.
- Schurz, Life of Clay, ii. 391, 392.
- Von Holst, iv. 65-75.

Perry's Japan Expedition
- Bryant & Gay, iv. 402.
- Haswell, Treaties and Conventions, Text of Treaty, 597-599.
- Johnston, 273.
- Lalor, Cyclopædia, ii. 632.
- Montgomery, 271.
- Patton, ii. 845.
- Rhodes, ii. 8, Note.
- Schouler, v. 255, 314.
- Thomas, 255.

The Filibuster Expedition against Cuba
- Fiske, Hist. of U.S., 340.
- Johnston, 273.
- Lalor, Cyclopædia, ii. 184.
- Patton, ii. 840, 841.
- Rhodes, i. 216-222.
- Sargent, Public Men and Events, ii. 380, 381.
- Schouler, v. 215-218.
- Thomas, 259.
- Von Holst, iv. 45-63.

Deaths of Clay and Webster
Their Characters
Clay
  The Southern Whig
  The Great Compromiser
  The Champion of Protection
- Blaine, i. 106-108.
- Fiske, Hist. of U.S., 339.
- Johnston, 267.
- Lodge, Life of Webster, 343-356.
- Montgomery, 269.
- Patton, ii. 841, 842.
- Rhodes, i. 261, 285-289.

Deaths of Clay and Webster
(Continued)

The most popular of all Americans

Webster
The Northern Whig
The Defender of the Constitution
The Ardent Advocate of the Union

- Sargent, Public Men and Events, ii. 384, 385, 391, 392, 393.
- Schouler, v. 245, 246.
- Schurz, Life of Clay, ii. 405-414.
- Thomas, 250, 253.
- Von Holst, iv. 203-205.
- Wilson, Epochs Am. History, 179.

Election of the Fourteenth President Franklin Pierce
Death of the Whig Party

"A second instance of a 'dark horse.'"
Fiske.

- Blaine, i. 102-105.
- Bryant & Gay, iv. 402, 403.
- Eggleston, 295.
- Greeley, i. 222-224.
- Higginson, 282.
- Irving-Fiske, 552.
- Johnston, Hist. Am. Politics, 156.
- Johnston, 269.
- Lalor, Cyclopædia, ii. 58; iii. 1107.
- Montgomery, 269, 270.
- Nicolay & Hay, Life of Lincoln, i. 332.
- Patton, ii. 842, 843.
- Richardson, 402, 403.
- Rhodes, i. 247-260, 277, 285.
- Schouler, v. 239-242, 249, 250.
- Sheldon, 371.
- Stanwood, Presidential Elections, 178-191.
- Thomas, 254.
- Von Holst, iv. 154-164, 167-172, 225-231.
- Wilson, Epochs Am. History, 178, 179.
- Wilson, Rise and Fall of Slave Power, ii. 360-377.

"Uncle Tom's Cabin"

- Coffin, Building the Nation, 397, 398.
- Draper, History of Civil War, i. 420.
- Eggleston, 296.
- Fiske, Hist. of U.S., 339, 340.
- Irving-Fiske, 551.

Period of Slavery Agitation

"Uncle Tom's Cabin"
(*Continued*)

- Montgomery, 268, 269.
- Rhodes, i. 278-285.
- Schouler, v. 247.
- Von Holst, iv. 237-243.
- Wilson, Epochs Am. History, 181.
- Wilson, Rise and Fall of Slave Power, ii. 519.

Case of Anthony Burns

"Rendition of Anthony Burns."
John G. Whittier.

- Bryant & Gay, iv. 400.
- Coffin, Building the Nation, 401, 402.
- Greeley, Am. Conflict, i. 215, 220, Note.
- Higginson, 281.
- Lalor, Cyclopædia, ii. 316.
- Rhodes, i. 500-506.
- Richardson, 418.
- Schouler, v. 294-296.
- Smith, Goldwin, 233.
- Von Holst, v. 61-63.
- Wilson, Rise and Fall of Slave Power, 435-441.

Administration of Franklin Pierce 1853-1857

Kansas-Nebraska Bill

Repeal of Missouri Compromise. Squatter or Popular Sovereignty.

"In its ultimate and unexpected consequences, one of the most far-reaching legislative acts in American History."
Johnston.

"That Congress shall neither legislate slavery into any territory or State, nor out of the same; but the

- Blaine, i. 111-117.
- Bryant & Gay, iv. 405-408.
- Draper, Hist. of the Civil War, i. 495.
- Eggleston, 298, 299.
- Fiske, Hist. of U.S., 340-342.
- Greeley, Am. Conflict, i. 228-235.
- Higginson, 282.
- Irving-Fiske, 552, 553.
- Johnston, Hist. Am. Politics, 159.
- Johnston, 274, 275.
- Lalor, Cyclopædia, ii. 667-670.
- Montgomery, 271, 272.
- Nicolay & Hay, Life of Lincoln, i. 337-351.
- Patton, ii. 846, 847.
- Rhodes, i. 439-459, 475, 480-489.
- Richardson, 419, 420.
- Schouler, v. 280-284, 285-289.

Kansas-Nebraska Bill
(Continued)
people shall be left free to regulate their domestic concerns in their own way, subject only to the Constitution of the United States." *Rhodes.*

- Sheldon, 299, 300.
- Smith, Goldwin, 234.
- Spring, Am. Commonwealths, Kansas, 1-16.
- Stanwood, Presidential Elections, 192.
- Thomas, 256.
- Von Holst, iv. 290-324.
- Wilson, Epochs Am. History, 182-185.
- Wilson, Rise and Fall of Slave Power, ii. 378-405.

Rise of the "Know-Nothing" or American Party

- Blaine, i. 117.
- Bryant & Gay, iv. 416, 417.
- Eggleston, 298.
- Fiske, Hist. of U.S., 344, 350.
- Higginson, 285.
- Johnston, 274.
- Lalor, Cyclopædia, i. 85-89.
- Montgomery, 270, Note i.
- Patton, ii. 850.
- Rhodes, ii. 50-57, 89-92.
- Sargent, Public Men and Events, 228-231.
- Schouler, v. 304-308.
- Smith, Goldwin, 215-217, 237.
- Thomas, 257.
- Von Holst, v. 79-89, 91-96, 123-130.
- Wilson, Epochs Am. History, 180, 187, 190, 193.
- Wilson, ii. 419-434.

The Gadsden Purchase
Price $10,000,000.

- Blaine, ii. 340.
- Higginson, 284.
- Johnston, 259.
- Lalor, Cyclopædia, i. 98.
- Montgomery, 270, Note.
- Patton, ii. 844.
- Rhodes, ii. 7.
- Schouler, v. 296.
- Sheldon, 371.
- Thomas, 241, Note.
- Von Holst, v. 6-9.

Period of Slavery Agitation

Gadsden Purchase
(Continued)
- Wilson, Epochs Am. History, 189.
- Winsor, vii. 553.

The Ostend Manifesto
- Eggleston, 300, Note.
- Fiske, Hist. of U.S., 340.
- Greeley, Am. Conflict, i. 273-276.
- Johnston, 273.
- Lalor, Cyclopædia, iii. 36.
- Rhodes, ii. 38-44.
- Schouler, v. 312-315.
- Smith, Goldwin, 215.
- Thomas, 259, 260.
- Von Holst, v. 36-50.
- Wilson, Epochs Am. History, 189, 190.
- Wilson, Rise and Fall of Slave Power, ii. 611-614.

The Struggle for Kansas
- Blaine, i. 119-122.
- Bryant & Gay, iv. 408-416.
- Coffin, Building the Nation, 407-414.
- Draper, Hist. of the Civil War, i. 414-417.
- Fiske, Hist. of U.S., 343.
- Greeley, Am. Conflict, i. 235-241, 243-245.
- Higginson, 282-284.
- Irving-Fiske, 554.
- Johnston, 276, 277.
- Lalor, Cyclopædia, ii. 665, 666.
- Montgomery, 272, 273.
- Nicolay & Hay, Life of Lincoln, i. 393-407.
- Patton, ii. 847, 848.
- Rhodes, ii. 78-87, 98-103.
- Richardson, 421-425.
- Schouler, v. 320-333.
- Sheldon, 299-303.
- Smith, Goldwin, 235, 236.
- Spring, Am. Commonwealths, Kansas, 23-62.
- Thomas, 260-263.
- Von Holst, v. 145-185.
- Wilson, Epochs Am. History, 185, 186.
- Wilson, Rise and Fall of Slave Power, ii. 462-474.

Rise of the Republican Party

Formed on the principle of no further extension of slavery.

- Blaine, i. 118, 126, 127.
- Bryant & Gay, iv. 421.
- Bryce, Am. Commonwealths, ii. 14.
- Coffin, Building the Nation, 414.
- Eggleston, 299.
- Fiske, Hist. of U.S., 342, 343.
- Greeley, Am. Conflict, i. 246, 247.
- Higginson, 279-285.
- Irving-Fiske, 553, 554.
- Johnston, 275, 276.
- Lalor, Cyclopædia, iii. 597, 598.
- Montgomery, 273, Note ii.
- Nicolay & Hay, Life of Lincoln, ii. 23-25.
- Patton, ii. 856.
- Rhodes, i. 490; ii. 45-49.
- Richardson, 426.
- Schouler, v. 303, 304, 349, 350.
- Sheldon, 300, 371.
- Smith, Goldwin, 214, 215.
- Thomas, 263.
- Von Holst, v. 130-133.
- Wilson, Epochs Am. History, 188.
- Wilson, Rise and Fall of Slave Power, ii. 406-418.
- Winsor, vii. 288.

The Assault on Charles Sumner

- Blaine, i. 129.
- Bryant & Gay, iv. 419-421.
- Coffin, Building the Nation, 414.
- Fiske, Hist. of U.S., 343, 344.
- Greeley, Am. Conflict, i. 229-300.
- Grimke, Life of Sumner, 278-285, 291.
- Irving-Fiske, 544.
- Johnston, 277, 278.
- Lalor, Cyclopædia, i. 310; iii. 833.
- Montgomery, 274.
- Nicolay & Hay, Life of Lincoln, ii. 41-57.
- Rhodes, ii. 139-150.
- Richardson, 420.
- Schouler, v. 343, 344.

Period of Slavery Agitation

The Assault on Charles Sumner (*Continued*)
- Sheldon, 371.
- Smith, Goldwin, 236.
- Thomas, 263.
- Von Holst, v. 314-328.
- Wilson, Rise and Fall of Slave Power, ii. 478-495.

Election of the Fifteenth President James Buchanan
- Blaine, i. 123-130.
- Bryant & Gay, iv. 421-424.
- Coffin, Building the Nation, 414.
- Eggleston, 300.
- Fiske, Hist. of U.S., 344, 345.
- Greeley, Am. Conflict, i. 245-248.
- Higginson, 285, 286.
- Irving-Fiske, 554.
- Johnston, History Am. Politics, 166-169.
- Johnston, 278.
- Lalor, Cyclopædia, i. 310-311; ii. 58.
- Montgomery, 275.
- Rhodes, ii. 171-186, 221-229, 235.
- Richardson, 426.
- Schouler, v. 351-357.
- Sheldon, 371.
- Smith, Goldwin, 237.
- Stanwood, Presidential Elections, 192-213.
- Thomas, 264.
- Von Holst, v. 436, 455-467.
- Wilson, Epochs Am. History, 190-193.
- Wilson, Rise and Fall of Slave Power, ii. 508-522.

Summary of Period of Slavery Agitation 1842-1856

1842
- The New Tariff Act.
- The Webster-Ashburton Treaty.
- Dorr's Rebellion.
- The Mormons.

1844
- The first Electric Telegraph.
- Election of James K. Polk.

1845
- Florida Admitted.
- Inauguration of President Polk.
- Texas Annexed to the United States.
- Texas Admitted.
- The Oregon Boundary Dispute.
- The first Sewing-Machine.
- The Texas Boundary Dispute.

1846
- Iowa Admitted.
- The New Tariff Act.
- The Mexican War in General.
- Taylor's Campaign in North Mexico.
- Fremont's California Campaign.
- Kearney's Campaign in New Mexico.
- The Wilmot Proviso.

1847
- Scott's Campaign in Central Mexico.

1848
- Treaty of Guadalupe Hidalgo.
- Discovery of Gold and the Emigration to California.
- Wisconsin Admitted.
- The Buffalo Convention.
- Formation of the Free-Soil Party.
- Election of Zachary Taylor and Millard Fillmore.

1849
- Inauguration of President Taylor.

1850
- Compromise of 1850.
- Death of Taylor and Succession of Fillmore.
- California Admitted.
- Webster's Seventh of March Speech.
- Passage of the Fugitive Slave Law.

1852
- Election of Franklin Pierce.
- Deaths of Clay and Webster.

1853
- Inauguration of President Pierce.
- Correspondence of Webster and Hülsemann.
- Perry's Japan Expedition.
- Filibuster Expedition against Cuba.

1854	"Uncle Tom's Cabin." Case of Anthony Burns. Rise of the Know-Nothing Party. The Gadsden Purchase. The Ostend Manifesto.
1855	The Struggle for Kansas.
1856	Election of James Buchanan. Rise of the Republican Party. Assault on Charles Sumner.

Period of Secession and Civil War 1856–1865

Administration of James Buchanan 1857-1861

**Kansas
The Topeka
and Lecompton
Constitutions**

> Blaine, i. 120, 121, 139-144.
> Bryant & Gay, iv. 410-415.
> Draper, Hist. of Civil War, i. 415, 416.
> Eggleston, 300.
> Fiske, Hist. of U.S., 347.
> Greeley, Am. Conflict, 240-245, 249, 250.
> Johnston, 277.
> Lalor, Cyclopædia, ii. 665, 666.
> Montgomery, 273, 274.
> Nicolay & Hay, Life of Lincoln, i. 425-437; ii. 90-118.
> Patton, ii. 851, 852.
> Rhodes, ii. 107, 150-168, 277-280, 291-293, 297.
> Richardson, 421-425.
> Schouler, v. 330-333, 344-348, 381-386.
> Sheldon, 301-303.
> Smith, Goldwin, 236.
> Spring, Am. Commonwealths, Kansas, 130-136, 210-236.
> Von Holst, v. 168; vi. 65-70, 80-94.
> Wilson, Epochs Am. History, 186, 199, 200.
> Wilson, Rise and Fall of Slave Power, ii. 469-477, 534-547.

**The Dred Scott
Decision**

"It declared the slave a 'thing' without rights, the Mis-

> Blaine, i. 130-135.
> Bryant & Gay, iv. 347, 424, 425.
> Draper, Hist. of Civil War, i. 336, 407, 408.
> Eggleston, 301.
> Fiske, Hist. of U.S., 346.

Period of Secession and Civil War 81

The Dred Scott Decision
(Continued)

souri Compromise unconstitutional and void, and slave property carriable anywhere. It was the last attempt to settle the slave question by law."

- Greeley, Am. Conflict, i. 251-264.
- Higginson, 286.
- Irving-Fiske, 254, 255.
- Johnston, 288.
- Lalor, Cyclopædia, i. 838-841.
- Montgomery, 275, 276.
- Nicolay & Hay, Life of Lincoln, ii. 58-80.
- Patton, ii. 856.
- Rhodes, ii. 250-271.
- Schouler, v. 377-381.
- Sheldon, 372.
- Smith, Goldwin, 234, 235.
- Thomas, 264, 265.
- Von Holst, vi. 25-46.
- Wilson, Epochs Am. History, 197-199.
- Wilson, Rise and Fall of Slave Power, ii. 524-533.

Personal Liberty and Homestead Laws

- Coffin, Building the Nation, 424.
- Fiske, Hist. of U.S., 340.
- Johnston, Hist. Am. Politics, 177, 179.
- Nicolay & Hay, Life of Lincoln, iii. 17-34.
- Patton, ii. 871.
- Rhodes, ii. 73, 74, 352-354.
- Schouler, v. 318-320.
- Smith, Goldwin, 233.
- Thomas, 251.
- Von Holst, v. 66-70.
- Wilson, Epochs Am. History, 208.
- Wilson, Rise and Fall of Slave Power, ii. 639, 640, 670.

Tariff and Financial Panic of 1857

- Blaine, i. 196-199.
- Johnston, Hist. Am. Politics, 168.
- Johnston, 280.
- Lalor, Cyclopædia, iii. 864, 865.
- Montgomery, 276, 277.
- Rhodes, ii. 281.
- Schouler, v. 363, 364, 386-389.
- Taussig, Tariff History, 115, 116, 157.

Tariff and Financial Panic of 1857 *(Continued)*	Thomas, 266. Von Holst, vi. 99, 100, 116-120, 124, 125. Wilson, Epochs Am. History, 196, 197.
The Mormon Rebellion	Bryant, iv. 427, 428. Coffin, Building the Nation, 446-449. Johnston, 281. Lalor, Cyclopædia, iii. 1044-1046. Montgomery, 250. Schouler, v. 403-406. Sheldon, 372. Thomas, 266. Von Holst, vi. 129-144.
The Lincoln-Douglass Debates "They marked an era; their influence and effect were co-extensive with the Republic." *Blaine.*	Blaine, i. 144-149. Fiske, Hist. of U.S., 347-349. Greeley, Am. Conflict, i. 301, 302. Lalor, Cyclopædia, ii. 770. Morse, Life of Lincoln, i. 111-160. Nicolay & Hay, Life of Lincoln, ii. 135-155. Rhodes, ii. 313-338. Richardson, 420. Schouler, v. 410-414. Von Holst, vi. 286-296. Wilson, Epochs Am. History, 201, 202. Wilson, Rise and Fall of Slave Power, i. 566-577.

Minnesota admitted, 1858.

John Brown's Raid	Blaine, i. 154-156. Bryant & Gay, iv. 429-431. Draper, Hist. of the Civil War, i. 525-527. Eggleston, 301. Fiske, Hist. of U.S., 349, 350. Greeley, Am. Conflict, i. 288-299. Higginson, 286-289. Irving-Fiske, 556. Johnston, 289. Lalor, Cyclopædia, i. 310. Montgomery, 278, 279.

Period of Secession and Civil War 83

John Brown's Raid
(Continued)

- Nicolay & Hay, Life of Lincoln, ii. 190-213.
- Patton, ii. 852-854.
- Pollard, Lost Cause, 70-74.
- Rhodes, ii. 383-416.
- Richardson, 426-431.
- Schouler, v. 437-444.
- Sheldon, 305-308.
- Smith, Goldwin, 237, 238.
- Thomas, 268.
- Wilson, Epochs Am. History, 202-204.
- Wilson, Rise and Fall of Slave Power, ii. 587-600.

Split in the Democratic Party and the Charleston Convention

- Blaine, i. 150-153, 157-164.
- Bryant & Gay, iv. 432, 433.
- Coffin, Building the Nation, 468, 469.
- Draper, Hist. of the Civil War, i. 496-502.
- Eggleston, 301, 302.
- Fiske, Hist. of U.S., 350.
- Greeley, Am. Conflict, i. 309-319.
- Irving-Fiske, 556, 557.
- Johnston, Hist. Am. Politics, 179-181.
- Johnston, 289-290.
- Lalor, Cyclopædia, i. 781, 782.
- Nicolay & Hay, Life of Lincoln, ii. 227-242.
- Patton, ii. 869.
- Pollard, Lost Cause, 66, 67.
- Rhodes, ii. 440-454.
- Richardson, 431, 432.
- Schouler, v. 454-457.
- Sheldon, 314.
- Smith, Goldwin, 238.
- Thomas, 268.
- Wilson, Epochs Am. History, 200, 204, 206.
- Wilson, Rise and Fall of Slave Power, ii. 673-688.

Oregon admitted, 1859.

Handbook of American History

Election of the Sixteenth President Abraham Lincoln
- Blaine. i. 166-172.
- Bryant & Gay, iv. 433, 434.
- Coffin, Building the Nation, 468-472.
- Draper, Hist. of the Civil War, i. 503-506.
- Eggleston, 301, 302.
- Fiske, Hist. of U.S., 350.
- Greeley, Am. Conflict, i. 328, 329.
- Irving-Fiske, 557.
- Johnston, Hist. Am. Politics, 181, 182.
- Johnston, 291.
- Lalor, Cyclopædia, ii. 59.
- Morse, Life of Lincoln, i. 164-179.
- Nicolay & Hay, Life of Lincoln, ii. 255-295.
- Patton, ii. 869, 870.
- Rhodes, ii. 477-480, 483-489, 500-502.
- Richardson, 433-435.
- Schouler, v. 457-469.
- Sheldon, 314-317.
- Smith, Goldwin, 238-241.
- Stanwood, Presidential Elections, 214-235.
- Thomas, 269.
- Wilson, Epochs Am. History, 204-210.
- Wilson, Rise and Fall of Slave Power, ii. 689-764.

Petroleum, or coal oil, discovered in Pennsylvania, 1859.

Secession of the Seven Cotton States
- Blaine, i. 216-221.
- Bryant & Gay, iv. 435-437.
- Coffin, Building the Nation, 472.
- Coffin, Drumbeat of the Nation, 36, 39.
- De Trobriand, 1-30.
- Draper, Hist. of the Civil War. i. 510-516.
- Eggleston, 304, 305.
- Fiske, Hist. of U.S., 351.
- Greeley, Am. Conflict, i. 328-351.
- Higginson, 289.
- Irving-Fiske, 559, 560.
- Johnston, Hist. Am. Politics, 182, 183.
- Johnston, 292, 293.
- Lalor, Cyclopædia, iii. 699-700.

Period of Secession and Civil War

Secession of the Seven Cotton States *(Continued)*

- Morse, Life of Lincoln, i. 184-187.
- Nicolay & Hay, Life of Lincoln, iii. 1-16.
- Nicolay, Outbreak of the Rebellion, 1-16.
- Patton, ii. 872, 879.
- Pollard, Lost Cause, 83, 84.
- Richardson, 433-435.
- Schouler, v. 474-480, 488-490.
- Sheldon, 314-321.
- Smith, Goldwin, 241-244.
- Stevens, War between the States, ii. 300-309.
- Thomas, 269, 270.
- Wilson, Epochs Am. History, 210-212.
- Wilson, Rise and Fall of Slave Power, iii. 2-10, 109-117.

Summary of Period of Secession and Civil War to January, 1861

1857
- Inauguration of President Buchanan.
- The Dred Scott Decision.
- The Topeka and Lecompton Constitutions.
- Personal Liberty and Homestead Laws.
- The Tariff and Panic of 1857.
- The Mormon Rebellion.

1858
- The Lincoln-Douglas Debates.
- Minnesota Admitted.

1859
- John Brown's Raid.
- Split in the Democratic Party.
- Oregon Admitted.
- Petroleum Discovered.

1860
- Election of Abraham Lincoln.
- Secession of the Seven Cotton States.

Kansas admitted, 1861.

The Policy of Hesitation
The Crittenden Compromise

- Blaine, i. 222-229, 239-241.
- Bryant & Gay, iv. 438-440.
- Draper, i. 518-520, 522-524, 554-556.
- Eggleston, 305, 306.

86 Handbook of American History

The Policy of Hesitation
The Crittenden Compromise
(Continued)

- Fiske, Hist. of U.S., 351, 352.
- Greeley, Am. Conflict, i. 355, 356, 368-372, 376-382.
- Johnston, Hist. Am. Politics, 183, 184.
- Johnston, 296.
- Lalor, Cyclopædia, i. 553, 554.
- Montgomery, 283.
- Morse, Life of Lincoln, i. 202, 203.
- Nicolay & Hay, Life of Lincoln, iii. 69, 77-80, 224-227.
- Patton, ii. 873.
- Schouler, v. 471-474, 504-507.
- Sheldon, 320, 321.
- Smith, Goldwin, 244-247.
- Stevens, War between the States, ii. 300-309.
- Thomas, 272, 273.
- Wilson, Epochs Am. History, 213-216.
- Wilson, Rise and Fall of Slave Power, iii. 43-59, 71-95.

The Morrill Tariff of 1861

- Blaine, i. 399-401.
- Fiske, Hist. of U.S., 407.
- Johnston, History of Am. Politics, 185-189.
- Johnston, 336.
- Lalor, Cyclopædia, iii. 865.
- Nicolay & Hay, Life of Lincoln, iii. 243.
- Patton, ii. 971.
- Schouler, v. 503.
- Taussig, Tariff History of U.S., 158-161.
- Thomas, 304.

Establishment of the Confederate Government February 1861

- Blaine, i. 294, 295.
- Bryant & Gay, iv. 440, 441.
- Comte de Paris, History of the Civil War, i. 129.
- Draper, i. 528-536.
- Eggleston, 306.
- Fiske, Hist. of U.S., 351.
- Greeley, Am. Conflict, i. 414-416.

Period of Secession and Civil War

Establishment of the Confederate Government February 1861 (*Continued*)

- Higginson, 289-290.
- Irving-Fiske, 560.
- Johnston, 293, 294.
- Lalor, Cyclopædia, i. 566, 567, 569; iii. 998.
- Moore, Rebellion Record, xii. 42-53.
- Morse, Life of Lincoln, i. 205, 206.
- Nicolay & Hay, Life of Lincoln, iii. 195-204.
- Nicolay, The Outbreak of the Rebellion, 37-44.
- Patton, ii. 879.
- Richardson, 434.
- Schouler, v. 490-492.
- Sheldon, 322-325.
- Thomas, 271, 272.
- Wilson, Epochs Am. History, 211.
- Wilson, Rise and Fall of Slave Power, iii. 117-126.

First Administration of Abraham Lincoln 1861-1865

President Lincoln

- Blaine, i. 279-283, 290, 291.
- Bryant & Gay, iv. 445.
- Coffin, Drumbeat of the Nation, 23-27.
- Draper, ii. 13-17.
- Fiske, Hist. of U.S., 352, 353.
- Greeley, Am. Conflict, i. 418-428.
- Johnston, 297.
- Montgomery, 285, 286.
- Morse, Life of Lincoln, i. 227-231.
- Nicolay & Hay, Life of Lincoln, iii. 245, 246, 317, 318, 342-344.
- Nicolay, Outbreak of the Rebellion, 45-50.
- Patton, ii. 880, 881.
- Richardson, 436.
- Schouler, v. 497, 498, 501, 502.
- Sheldon, 321.
- Smith, Goldwin, 250-253.
- Wilson, Epochs of Am. History, 216-218.
- Wilson, Rise and Fall of Slave Power, iii. 179-183.

Handbook of American History

The Fall of Sumter April 13, 1861

- Abbott, History of the Civil War, i. 88-91.
- Battles and Leaders of the Civil War, i. 50-81.
- Blaine, i. 296.
- Bryant & Gay, iv. 442-447.
- Coffin, Building the Nation, 473.
- Coffin, Drumbeat of the Nation, 44-47.
- Comte de Paris, i. 138, 139.
- De Trobriand, 53, 54.
- Draper, ii. 58-64.
- Drumbeat of the Nation, 42-47.
- Eggleston, 306, 307.
- Fiske, Hist. of U.S., 356.
- Greeley, Am. Conflict, i. 440-447.
- Higginson, 290, 291.
- Irving-Fiske, 560.
- Johnston, 297-299.
- Lalor, Cyclopædia, iii. 533.
- Lossing, Hist. of the Civil War, i. 310-334.
- Montgomery, 286-288.
- Moore, Rebellion Record, i. 52-59.
- Nicolay & Hay, Life of Lincoln, iv. 49-63.
- Nicolay, Outbreak of the Rebellion, 56-68.
- Patton, ii. 883, 884.
- Richardson, 437-440.
- Schouler, vi.
- Smith, Goldwin, 253.
- Thomas, 274, 275.
- Wilson, Epochs Am. History, 218.
- Wilson, Rise and Fall of Slave Power, iii. 208-210.

The Call to Arms

- Battles and Leaders, i. 86.
- Blaine, i. 297, 298.
- Bryant & Gay, iv. 447.
- Coffin, Drumbeat of the Nation, 48.
- Comte de Paris, i. 140.
- Draper, ii. 70.
- Eggleston, 307.
- Fiske, Hist. of U.S., 356.

Period of Secession and Civil War

The Call to Arms
(Continued)

- Greeley, Am. Conflict, i. 453, 454.
- Higginson, 294.
- Irving-Fiske, 560.
- Johnston, 299.
- Montgomery, 288.
- Morse, Life of Lincoln, i. 251-254.
- Nicolay & Hay, Life of Lincoln, iv. 76, 77.
- Nicolay, Outbreak of the Rebellion, 69-77.
- Patton, ii. 885, 886.
- Richardson, 440, 443.
- Schouler, vi.
- Sheldon, 328-330.
- Smith, Goldwin, 256.
- Thomas, 277, 278.
- Wilson, Epochs Am. History, 218.
- Wilson, Rise and Fall of Slave Power, iii. 212-216.

Secession of four other States Virginia North Carolina Tennessee and Arkansas

- Blaine, i. 300-304.
- Bryant & Gay, iv. 448.
- Comte de Paris, i. 142, 149, 158.
- Draper, ii. 81.
- Eggleston, 307.
- Fiske, Hist. of U.S., 357.
- Greeley, Am. Conflict, i. 458, 461, 468, 473, 481, 482, 486, 489.
- Irving-Fiske, 561.
- Johnston, 301.
- Montgomery, 289.
- Nicolay & Hay, Life of Lincoln, iv. 104, 162, 183, 247-253.
- Nicolay, Outbreak of the Rebellion, 82, 83, 115, 126-129, 130.
- Pollard, Lost Cause, 82-99.
- Schouler, vi.
- Stevens, War between the States, ii. 312-333.
- Thomas, 278.
- Wilson, Epochs Am. History, 219.
- Wilson, Rise and Fall of the Slave Power, iii. 137-140, 144-146.

90   *Handbook of American History*

Congress called in Special Session Its War Measures

- Blaine, i. 313-315, 324, 332-337.
- Comte de Paris, i. 218-220.
- Draper, ii. 173-180, 182-185.
- Greeley, Am. Conflict, i. 555, 559-562, 572.
- Johnston, 303.
- Morse, Life of Lincoln, i. 291-298.
- Nicolay & Hay, Life of Lincoln, iv. 370-384.
- Patton, ii. 903.
- Schouler, vi.
- Wilson, Epochs Am. History, 219-221.
- Wilson, Rise and Fall of the Slave Power, iii. 220-231.

First Battle of Bull Run July 21, 1861

- Abbott, Battlefields of '61, 103-135.
- Battles and Leaders, i. 198-227.
- Blaine, i. 337, 338.
- Bryant & Gay, iv. 451-454.
- Coffin, Drumbeat of the Nation, 86-103.
- Comte de Paris, i. 231-256.
- Draper, ii. 114-130.
- Eggleston, 312.
- Fiske, Hist. of U.S., 358.
- Greeley, Am. Conflict, i. 539-547.
- Higginson, 296, 297.
- Irving-Fiske, 561.
- Johnston, 304.
- Lossing, i. 584-608.
- Montgomery, 292, 293.
- Moore, Rebellion Record, xii. 68-80.
- Morse, Life of Lincoln, i. 298-302.
- Nicolay & Hay, Life of Lincoln, iv. 343-357.
- Nicolay, Outbreak of the Rebellion, 181-196.
- Patton, ii. 894-897.
- Richardson, 457-461.
- Schouler, vi.
- Sheldon, 331-333.
- Thomas, 282-284.
- Wilson, Epochs Am. History, 221.

Period of Secession and Civil War

The Affair of the Trent

Battles and Leaders, ii. 118, 135-142.
Blaine, i. 580-587.
Bryant & Gay, iv. 459-461.
Comte de Paris, i. 464-472.
Draper, ii. 540-546.
Eggleston, 350, 351.
Fiske, Hist. of U.S., 358, 359.
Greeley, Am. Conflict, i. 606-608.
Higginson, 297, 298.
Irving-Fiske, 562.
Johnston, 306.
Lalor, Cyclopædia, iii. 949.
Maclay, Hist. of the Navy, ii. 236, 237.
Montgomery, 294, 295.
Moore, Rebellion Record, iii. 321-336.
Morse, Life of Lincoln, i. 380-387.
Nicolay & Hay, Life of Lincoln, v. 21-41.
Patton, ii. 907, 908.
Porter, Naval Hist. of the Civil War, 63-74.
Richardson, 470, 471.
Schouler, vi.
Sheldon, 373.
Thomas, 285, 286.
Wilson, Epochs Am. History, 222.

Summary of the Events of 1861

March
- Inauguration of President Lincoln.
- Kansas Admitted.

April
- Attack on Sumter. First Bloodshed at Baltimore. Call for Volunteers. Virginia, North Carolina, Tennessee, Arkansas, join the Confederacy.
- Richmond becomes the Capital of the Confederacy.
- President Lincoln proclaims the Blockade.

May
- Confederates busy at forming Lines of Defence.

Handbook of American History

July
: Meeting of Congress. $500,000,000 voted to carry on the War. The President granted War Powers. Battle of Bull Run. McClellan appointed Commander-in-chief of the Army. Battle of Wilson's Creek, Mo. Union Forces capture Fort Hatteras, N.C.

October
: Battle of Ball's Bluff, Va. Union Forces capture Port Royal, S.C.

November
: Trent Affair.

Campaign of 1862

First Battle of Ironclads
The Monitor and Merrimac
March 8, 1862

Battles and Leaders, i. 692-711.
Blaine, i. 358, 359.
Bryant & Gay, iv. 464, 465.
Coffin, Drumbeat of the Nation, 165-172.
Comte de Paris, i. 595-608.
Draper, ii. 418-425.
Eggleston, 324, 325.
Fiske, Hist. of U.S., 359-362.
Greeley, Am. Conflict, ii. 116-119.
Irving-Fiske, 565.
Johnston, 313, 314.
Maclay, Hist. of the Navy, ii. 282-324.
Montgomery, 295, 296.
Moore, Rebellion Record, iv. 270-280; ix. 241-245.
Morse, Life of Lincoln, i. 356, 357.
Nicolay & Hay, Life of Lincoln, v. 218-238.
Patton, ii. 932-936.
Porter, 119-133.
Richardson, 480-482.
Schouler, vi.
Sheldon, 335-337, 373.
Smith, Goldwin, 272.
Thomas, 289.
Wilson, Epochs Am. History, 229.

Period of Secession and Civil War

The Campaign of 1862 in the West
Battles of
 Fort Henry
 Fort Donelson
 Shiloh
 Perryville and Murfreesboro

- Abbott, Battlefields of '61, 181-211, 239-261.
- Battles and Leaders, i. 368-372, 401-428, 465-486; iii. 31-45.
- Blaine, i. 361, 362.
- Bryant & Gay, iv. 515-518, 522-525, 531, 534, 535.
- Coffin, Drumbeat of the Nation, 136-157, 196-217, 359-363, 420-433.
- Comte de Paris, i. 481-497, 538-555; ii. 381-394, 500-534.
- Draper, ii. 262-271, 284-302, 357, 360-365.
- Eggleston, 312, 314, 315, 331.
- Fiske, Hist. of U.S., 362-364.
- Force, Campaigns of the Civil War, 28-32, 33-60, 122-181.
- Greeley, ii. 45-51, 58-71, 217-222, 270-282.
- Higginson, 302.
- Irving-Fiske, 563, 564, 568.
- Johnston, 307-311.
- Montgomery, 296-298, 304.
- Moore, Rebellion Record, xii. 414-456.
- Nicolay & Hay, Life of Lincoln, v. 120-122, 185-200, 303-335; vi. 273-296.
- Patton, ii. 922-926, 967, 968.
- Porter, 141-144, 149-157.
- Richardson, 472-477, 482-486.
- Schouler, vi.
- Sheldon, 373.
- Thomas, 287, 288, 293.
- Wilson, Epochs Am. History, 223, 224.

Farragut's Capture of New Orleans April 25, 1862

- Abbott, Battlefields of '61, 262-277.
- Battles and Leaders, ii. 22-54.
- Blaine, i. 359.
- Bryant & Gay, iv. 526-529.
- Coffin, Drumbeat of the Nation, 218-225.
- Comte de Paris, ii. 153-173.

Farragut's Capture of New Orleans April 25, 1862 (*Continued*)

- Draper, ii. 327-341.
- Eggleston, 326.
- Fiske, Hist. of U.S., 364.
- Greeley, Am. Conflict, ii. 81-101
- Higginson, 303, 304.
- Irving-Fiske, 564.
- Johnston, 315, 316.
- Maclay, History of the Navy, ii. 364-410.
- Montgomery, 299, 300.
- Nicolay & Hay, Life of Lincoln, v. 252-272.
- Patton, ii. 926-929.
- Porter, Naval History, 175-188.
- Richardson, 490-493.
- Schouler, vi.
- Sheldon, 338.
- Thomas, 290.
- Wilson, Epochs Am. History, 224.

The Peninsula Campaign April-July 1862 From Yorktown to Malvern Hill

- Abbott, Battlefields of '61, 282-355.
- Battles and Leaders, ii. 160-187.
- Blaine, i. 363-367.
- Bryant & Gay, iv. 467-491.
- Coffin, Drumbeat of the Nation, 236-276.
- Comte de Paris, ii. 6-28, 52-72, 85-104, 107-148.
- De Trobriand, 261-289.
- Draper, ii. 378-389, 397-417.
- Eggleston, 318, 319.
- Fiske, Hist. of U.S., 365-367.
- Greeley, Am. Conflict, ii. 140-169.
- Higginson, 298.
- Irving-Fiske, 565-567.
- Johnston, 319-321.
- McClellan's Own Story, 377-384, 433-437.
- Montgomery, 301, 302.
- Moore, Rebellion Record, xii. 245-251, 272-279, 550-594.
- Morse, Life of Lincoln, ii. 37-66.
- Nicolay & Hay, Life of Lincoln, v. 358-391, 413-440.

Period of Secession and Civil War

The Peninsula Campaign April-July 1862 From Yorktown to Malvern Hill (*Continued*)
- Patton, ii. 940-952.
- Richardson, 498, 499.
- Schouler, vi.
- Sheldon, 373.
- Thomas, 290, 291.
- Walker, History of the Second Corps. 14-87.
- Webb, The Peninsula, 35-82, 93-167.
- Wilson, Epochs Am. History, 224, 225.

Lee's Campaign against Pope Battles of Cedar Mountain and Second Bull Run Summer 1862
- Battles and Leaders, ii. 449-494.
- Blaine, i. 448, 449.
- Bryant & Gay, iv. 492-498.
- Coffin, Drumbeat of the Nation, 278-297.
- Comte de Paris, ii. 250, 251, 256-261, 279-304.
- De Trobriand, 283-307.
- Draper, ii. 430-445.
- Eggleston, 319, 320.
- Fiske, Hist. of U.S., 368, 369.
- Greeley, Am. Conflict, ii. 172-189.
- Higginson, 298, 299.
- Irving-Fiske, 567.
- Johnston, 321.
- Montgomery, 303.
- Moore, Rebellion Record, v. 325-331, 342-361, 466-475.
- Morse, Life of Lincoln, ii. 74-80.
- Nicolay & Hay, Life of Lincoln, vi. 1-21.
- Patton, ii. 953-956.
- Richardson, 499, 500.
- Schouler, vi.
- Thomas, 292.
- Wilson, Epochs Am. History, 225, 226.

Lee invades Maryland Battle of Antietam Sept. 17, 1862
- Battles and Leaders, ii. 630-660.
- Blaine, i. 449, 450.
- Bryant & Gay, iv. 498-504.
- Coffin, Drumbeat of the Nation, 298-333.
- Coffin, Marching to Victory. 127-159.

96 Handbook of American History

Lee invades Maryland
Battle of Antietam Sept. 17, 1862
(Continued)

- Comte de Paris, ii. 309-325, 331-359.
- De Trobriand, 308-327.
- Draper, ii. 451-466.
- Eggleston, 320.
- Fiske, Hist. of U.S., 369, 370.
- Greeley, Am. Conflict, ii. 193-212.
- Higginson, 299.
- Irving-Fiske, 567.
- Johnston, 321, 322.
- Montgomery, 303, 304.
- Moore, Rebellion Record, v. 437-439; xii. 627-638.
- Morse, Life of Lincoln, ii. 83-87.
- Nicolay & Hay, Life of Lincoln, vi. 131-146.
- Palfrey, The Antietam and Fredericksburg, 42-135.
- Patton, ii. 957-960.
- Richardson, 504, 505.
- Schouler, vi.
- Sheldon, 373.
- Thomas, 293.
- Walker, Hist. of Second Corps, 87-127.
- Wilson, Epochs Am. History, 226.

Burnside at Fredericksburg Dec. 13, 1862

- Battles and Leaders, iii. 70-85.
- Blaine, i. 452.
- Bryant & Gay, iv. 508-511.
- Coffin, Drumbeat of the Nation, 393-414.
- Comte de Paris, ii. 575-599.
- Draper, ii. 468-474.
- Eggleston, 320.
- Fiske, Hist. of U.S., 373.
- Greeley, Am. Conflict, ii. 342-350.
- Higginson, 300.
- Johnston, 322.
- Montgomery, 304.
- Morse, Life of Lincoln, ii. 136, 137.
- Nicolay & Hay, Life of Lincoln, vi. 200-211.

Period of Secession and Civil War

Burnside at Fredericksburg Dec. 13, 1862
(Continued)
- Palfrey, The Antietam and Fredericksburg, 136-190.
- Patton, ii. 961, 962.
- Richardson, 507.
- Schouler, vi.
- Sheldon, 373.
- Thomas, 293.
- Wilson, Epochs Am. History, 226.

West Virginia admitted, Dec. 31, 1862.

Summary of the Events of 1862

January — Union Victory at Mill Springs, Ky.

February
- Capture of Fort Henry, Tenn.
- Capture of Roanoke Island, N.C.
- Capture of Fort Donelson, Tenn.

March
- Battle of Pea Ridge, Ark.
- Fight of the Monitor and Merrimac.

April
- Battle of Shiloh, Pittsburg Landing, Tenn. Death of Albert Sidney Johnston.
- Capture of Island No. 10.
- Fall of New Orleans.

May
- Siege of Yorktown, Va.
- Battle of Williamsburg, Va.
- Capture of Corinth, Miss. Battle of Fair Oaks, Va.
- Negroes begin to be organized as United States Troops.

June — The Seven Days' Battles near Richmond.

July — Battle of Malvern Hill.

August
- Pope's Campaign in Va. Second Bull Run Battle.

September
- Capture of Harper's Ferry by the Confederates.
- Battle of Antietam, Md.
- Bragg's Invasion of Kentucky.

Handbook of American History

October
- Battle of Perryville.
- President Lincoln announces his purpose to free the slaves.

December
- Battle of Fredericksburg, Va.
- First Attempt on Vicksburg, Miss.
- Battle of Murfreesboro, Tenn.

First Administration of Abraham Lincoln 1861-1865

Emancipation
Jan. 1, 1863

"The great Historic Event of the War."
Henry Wilson.

- Blaine, i. 445-447.
- Bryant & Gay, iv. 504, 543, 544.
- Coffin, Drumbeat of the Nation, 458, 459.
- Comte de Paris, ii. 739, 743-747.
- Draper, ii. 601-614.
- Eggleston, 325, 326.
- Fiske, Hist. of U.S., 371.
- Greeley, Am. Conflict, ii. 252-256.
- Higginson, 304, 305.
- Irving-Fiske, 569, 570.
- Johnston, 323, 324.
- Montgomery, 304, 305.
- Morse, Life of Lincoln, ii. 130-133.
- Nicolay & Hay, Life of Lincoln, vi. 147, 161, 162, 169, 171, 399-430.
- Patton, ii. 965, 970, 971.
- Richardson, 514-516.
- Schouler, vi.
- Sheldon, 340-342.
- Thomas, 294-296.
- Wilson, Epochs Am. History, 226, 227.
- Wilson, Rise and Fall of Slave Power, iii. 380-393.

The Campaign of 1862 in the East

Hooker at Chancellorsville
May 3, 1863

- Battles and Leaders, iii. 154-171.
- Blaine, i. 493, 494.
- Bryant & Gay, iv. 545-551.
- Coffin, Marching to Victory, 127-159.

Period of Secession and Civil War

Hooker at Chancellorsville May 3, 1863 (*Continued*)

- Comte de Paris, iii. 23-47, 53-72, 75-115.
- Doubleday, Chancellorsville, 5-74.
- Draper, iii. 106-124.
- Eggleston, 320, 321.
- Fiske, Hist. of U.S., 373.
- Greeley, Am. Conflict, ii. 352-365.
- Irving-Fiske, 570.
- Johnston, 326.
- Montgomery, 306.
- Morse, Life of Lincoln, ii. 140-142.
- Nicolay & Hay, Life of Lincoln, vii. 87-111.
- Patton, ii. 972-975.
- Richardson, 524-526.
- Schouler, vi.
- Sheldon, 343-345.
- Thomas, 298.
- Wilson, Epochs Am. History, 230.

Lee's Second Invasion of Maryland Battle of Gettysburg July 1-4, 1863

- Battles and Leaders, iii. 244-251, 267-284, 293-313, 369-385.
- Blaine, i. 495, 496.
- Bryant & Gay, iv. 551-557.
- Coffin, Marching to Victory, 200-282.
- Comte de Paris, iii. 538-694.
- Draper, iii. 136-152.
- Doubleday, Gettysburg, 117-210.
- Eggleston, 321.
- Fiske, Hist. of U.S., 373.
- Greeley, Am. Conflict, ii. 375-389.
- Higginson, 306, 307.
- Irving-Fiske, 570, 571.
- Johnston, 327, 328.
- Montgomery, 306, 307.
- Morse, Life of Lincoln, ii. 146-149.
- Nicolay & Hay, Life of Lincoln, vii. 197-281.
- Patton, ii. 976-984.
- Richardson, 527-529.
- Schouler, vi.
- Sheldon, 345, 346.
- Thomas, 298, 299.
- Wilson, Epochs Am. History, 230.

The Reopening of the Mississippi Sieges of Vicksburg and Port Hudson

- Battles and Leaders, iii. 493-539.
- Blaine, i. 496, 497.
- Bryant & Gay, iv. 557-559.
- Coffin, Marching to Victory, 283-315.
- Comte de Paris, iii. 349-402.
- Draper, iii. 25-56.
- Eggleston, 327, 328.
- Fiske, Hist. of U.S., 374.
- Greeley, American Conflict, ii. 286-316.
- Greene, The Mississippi, 135-233.
- Higginson, 307, 308.
- Irving-Fiske, 571.
- Johnston, 329, 330.
- Montgomery, 307-310.
- Morse, Life of Lincoln, ii. 157-162.
- Nicolay & Hay, Life of Lincoln, vii. 282-327.
- Patton, ii. 985-987.
- Richardson, 517-524.
- Schouler, vi.
- Sheldon, 346, 349.
- Thomas, 299.
- Wilson, Epochs Am. History, 230, 231.

The Tennessee Campaign of 1863 Battles of Chickamauga and Chattanooga

- Battles and Leaders, iii. 638-662, 679-709.
- Bryant & Gay, iv. 561-565.
- Cist, Army of the Cumberland, 193-229, 243-262.
- Coffin, Marching to Victory, 401-455.
- Comte de Paris, iv. 102-131, 134-178, 253-279, 280-315.
- Draper, iii. 67-74, 75-97.
- Eggleston, 331, 333, 334.
- Fiske, Hist. of U.S., 375, 378.
- Greeley, American Conflict, ii. 408-426, 434-446.
- Higginson, 308, 309.
- Irving-Fiske, 571, 572.
- Johnston, 332-334.
- Montgomery, 310, 311.

CALIFORNIA

Period of Secession and Civil War

The Tennessee
Campaign of
1863
Battles of
Chickamauga
and Chattanooga
(*Continued*)

- Moore, Rebellion Record, ii. 73; vii. 240-246; viii. 190-198; x. 324-334, 335-372.
- Morse, Life of Lincoln, ii. 165-167.
- Nicolay & Hay, Life of Lincoln, viii. 75-108, 121-157.
- Patton, ii. 993-996.
- Richardson, 540-543.
- Schouler, vi.
- Sheldon, 347, 348.
- Thomas, 300.
- Wilson, Epochs Am. History, 232.

How the Enormous
War Expenses
were paid The
Legal-Tender
Act Adoption
of National
Banking System
Feb. 25, 1863

The Government from 1862 to 1879 paid its bills in its own paper currency.

- Blaine, i. 411-429, 470-482.
- Comte de Paris, iii. 412-418.
- Draper, ii. 564-574; iii. 491, 492.
- Eggleston, 352.
- Johnston, 324.
- Lalor, Cyclopædia, i. 215, 217.
- Montgomery, 249.
- Nicolay & Hay, Life of Lincoln, vi. 230-237, 242-247.
- Schouler, vi.
- Thomas, 304, 306, 307.
- Wilson, Epochs Am. History, 232, 233.

The Draft and
Draft Riots

- Bryant & Gay, iv. 559, 560.
- Coffin, Marching to Victory, 321-328.
- Comte de Paris, iii. 407-412.
- Draper, iii. 437, 442-445.
- Greeley, ii. 487, 488, 501-508.
- Johnston, 337.
- Lalor, Cyclopædia, i. 836, 837.
- Montgomery, 310.
- Morse, Life of Lincoln, ii. 194-199.
- Nicolay & Hay, Life of Lincoln, vii. 3-26.
- Patton, ii. 989, 990.
- Richardson, 530-533.
- Schouler, vi.
- Sheldon, 374.
- Thomas, 303, 304.
- Wilson, Epochs Am. History, 228, 229.

Summary of the Events of 1863

January	The Emancipation Proclamation.
March	Draft Act passed, and the beginning of Conscription for the Union Army.
April	Confederates win at Fort Sumter.
May	Confederate Victory over Hooker at Chancellorsville.
June	West Virginia admitted as a new State. Lee invades Maryland a Second Time.
July	Federal Victory at Gettysburg. Fall of Vicksburg and Port Hudson. Morgan's Cavalry Raid in Ohio. Draft Riots for Three Days in New York. Battle of Helena, Ark.
September	Confederates win the Battle of Chickamauga.
October	Chattanooga besieged by the Confederates.
November	Siege of Knoxville, Tenn. Grant wins the Battles of Lookout Mountain and Missionary Ridge, at Chattanooga.

Campaign of 1864

The New Commanders
Grant appointed Lieutenant-General
Sherman commands the Army of the West

Battles and Leaders, iv. 97-99.
Blaine, i. 509-512.
Bryant & Gay, iv. 569, 570.
Coffin, Redeeming the Republic, 67-72
Draper, iii. 259-262.
Eggleston, 334.
Fiske, Hist. of U.S., 378.
Greeley, ii. 562-564.
Higginson, 311.
Irving-Fiske, 572.

Period of Secession and Civil War 103

The New Commanders
Grant appointed Lieutenant-General
Sherman commands the Army of the West
(*Continued*)

- Johnston, 338.
- Montgomery, 311.
- Morse, Life of Lincoln, ii. 277, 278.
- Nicolay & Hay, Life of Lincoln, viii. 334-343.
- Patton, ii. 998-1000.
- Richardson, 548.
- Schouler, vi.
- Sheldon, 354.
- Thomas, 311.
- Wilson, Epochs of Am. History, 234.

Grant's Campaign to the James

- Battles and Leaders, iv. 118-144, 213-220.
- Bryant & Gay, iv. 572-579.
- Coffin, Redeeming the Republic, 78-124.
- Draper, iii. 368-389.
- Eggleston, 338, 339.
- Fiske, Hist. of U.S., 378.
- Greeley, Am. Conflict, ii. 566-574, 577-582.
- Higginson, 311, 312.
- Humphreys, Virginia Campaign of '64 and '65, 18-118, 182-193.
- Irving-Fiske, 572.
- Johnston, 339-341.
- Montgomery, 312, 313.
- Morse, Life of Lincoln, ii. 279-282.
- Nicolay & Hay, Life of Lincoln, viii. 352-391, 400-407.
- Patton, ii. 1006-1011.
- Richardson, 549-552.
- Schouler, vi.
- Sheldon, 358, 359.
- Thomas, 312, 313.
- Wilson, Epochs Am. History, 234.

The Nine Months' Siege of Petersburg
The Battles of the Crater and Reams Station

- Battles and Leaders, iv. 533-537, 545-560.
- Bryant & Gay, iv. 589-594.
- Coffin, Redeeming the Republic, 312-334, 358-374.
- Draper, iii. 394-406, 414-419.
- Eggleston, 338-340.

The Nine Months' Siege of Petersburg The Battles of the Crater and Reams Station (*Continued*)	Greeley, Am. Conflict, ii. 583-598. Humphreys, 247-266, 268-321. Irving-Fiske, 572, 573. Johnston, 342. Montgomery, 315. Nicolay & Hay, Life of Lincoln, ix. 406-435. Patton, ii. 1013, 1014. Richardson, 356, 357. Schouler, vi. Sheldon, 359. Thomas, 314. Wilson, Epochs Am. History, 234.
Sheridan's Campaign against Early in the Shenandoah Valley Battles of Winchester Fisher's Hill and Cedar Creek	Battles and Leaders, iv. 500-521. Bryant & Gay, iv. 594, 595. Draper, iii. 406-414. Eggleston, 340-342. Fiske, Hist. of U.S., 378, 380. Greeley, American Conflict, ii. 607-615. Higginson, 312. Johnston, 342, 343. Montgomery, 314-316. Nicolay & Hay, Life of Lincoln, ix. 291-331. Patton, ii. 1011-1013. Pond, The Shenandoah, 111-242. Richardson, 554-556. Schouler, vi. Thomas, 313, 314. Wilson, Epochs Am. History, 234, 235.

Nevada admitted, 1864.

Sherman's Campaign from Chattanooga to Atlanta	Battles and Leaders, iv. 250-257, 260-274, 293-323. Bryant & Gay, iv. 579-583. Coffin, Redeeming the Republic, 199-259, 335-357, 401-426. Cox, Atlanta, 35-48, 70-88, 116-129, 163-187, 198-210. Draper, iii. 265-305. Eggleston, 334, 335.

Period of Secession and Civil War

Sherman's Campaign from Chattanooga to Atlanta
(*Continued*)

- Fiske, Hist. of U.S., 380.
- Greeley, Am. Conflict, ii. 625-633, 637-641.
- Higginson, 315.
- Irving-Fiske, 573.
- Johnston, 344-346.
- Montgomery, 316.
- Nicolay & Hay, Life of Lincoln, ix. 1-28, 263-274, 278-290.
- Patton, ii. 1000-1004.
- Richardson, 564-567.
- Schouler, vi.
- Thomas, 315.
- Wilson, Epochs Am. History, 235.

The March from Atlanta to the Sea
Capture of Savannah

- Battles and Leaders, iv. 566-666.
- Bryant & Gay, iv. 583-586.
- Cox, The March to the Sea, 21-61.
- Draper, iii. 310-339.
- Eggleston, 346.
- Fiske, Hist. of U.S., 381, 382.
- Greeley, Am. Conflict, ii. 689-695.
- Higginson, 315.
- Irving-Fiske, 574.
- Johnston, 347.
- Montgomery, 317-319.
- Nicolay & Hay, Life of Lincoln, ix. 478-494.
- Patton, ii. 1005.
- Richardson, 569-572.
- Schouler, vi.
- Sheldon, 355, 356.
- Thomas, 316-318.
- Wilson, Epochs Am. History, 235.

Hood's Sortie into Tennessee
Battles of Franklin and Nashville

- Battles and Leaders, iv. 440-464.
- Bryant & Gay, iv. 583.
- Cox, The March to the Sea, 81-136.
- Draper, iii. 343-357.
- Eggleston, 345, 346.
- Fiske, Hist. of U.S., 381.
- Greeley, ii. 677-687.

Hood's Sortie into Tennessee
Battles of Franklin and Nashville
(Continued)

- Irving-Fiske, 573, 574.
- Johnston, 346.
- Montgomery, 317, 318, 319.
- Nicolay & Hay, Life of Lincoln, x. 1-37.
- Patton, ii. 1016-1018.
- Richardson, 567-569.
- Schouler, vi.
- Thomas, 315, 316.
- Wilson, Epochs Am. History, 235.

Confederate Cruisers

The Duel of the Alabama and Kearsarge off Cherbourg, June 19, 1864.

- Battles and Leaders, iv. 600-614.
- Bryant & Gay, iv. 589.
- Draper, iii. 188-203.
- Eggleston, 351, 352.
- Fiske, Hist. of U.S., 359, 380.
- Greeley, Am. Conflict, ii. 641-649.
- Higginson, 312, 313.
- Irving-Fiske, 573.
- Johnston, 350, 351.
- Maclay, History of the Navy, ii. 553-573.
- Montgomery, 313.
- Nicolay & Hay, Life of Lincoln, ix. 128-153.
- Patton, ii. 1030, 1031.
- Porter, Naval History, 648-655.
- Richardson, 560-562.
- Schouler, vi.
- Thomas, 318, 319.
- Wilson, Epochs Am. History, 235.

The Battle of Mobile Bay Aug. 5, 1864

"I am going into Mobile Bay in the morning, if 'God is my Leader;' as I hope he is."
David G. Farragut.

- Battles and Leaders, iv. 379-400.
- Bryant & Gay, iv. 589.
- Draper, iii. 220-228.
- Fiske, Hist. of U.S., 380.
- Greeley, Am. Conflict, ii. 649-654.
- Higginson, 313, 314.
- Irving-Fiske, 573.
- Johnston, 349.
- Maclay, History of the Navy, ii. 456-483.
- Montgomery, 317.

Period of Secession and Civil War

The Battle of Mobile Bay Aug. 5, 1864 (*Continued*)
- Nicolay & Hay, Life of Lincoln, ix. 222-243.
- Patton, ii. 1014, 1015.
- Porter, Naval History, 565-578.
- Richardson, 562-564.
- Schouler, vi.
- Sheldon, 374.
- Thomas, 319.
- Wilson, Epochs Am. History, 236.

Reëlection of President Lincoln Andrew Johnson Vice-President
- Blaine, i. 513-532.
- Bryant & Gay, iv. 587.
- Draper, iii. 470-476.
- Eggleston, 353.
- Fiske, Hist. of U.S., 381.
- Greeley, Am. Conflict, ii. 658-660, 669-672.
- Irving-Fiske, 574, 575.
- Johnston, History of Am. Politics, 193, 194.
- Johnston, 352.
- Morse, Life of Lincoln, ii. 286-295.
- Nicolay & Hay, Life of Lincoln, ix. 52-78, 256-262, 351-384.
- Patton, ii. 1019, 1020.
- Richardson, 583.
- Schouler, vi.
- Stanwood, Presidential Elections, 236-252.
- Thomas, 321-322.
- Wilson, Epochs Am. History, 236, 237.
- Wilson, Rise and Fall of Slave Power, iii. 549-551, 559-561.

Summary of the Events of 1864

March
- Grant made Commander-in-Chief.
- Sherman in Command in the West.

April
- Red River Expedition, Louisiana.
- Confederate Capture of Fort Pillow, Tenn.

Handbook of American History

May	Battle of the Wilderness, Va. Battle of Spottsylvania, Va. Union Victories at Resaca and Dallas, Ga.
June	Battle of Cold Harbor, Va. Siege of Petersburg begins. Duel of Kearsarge and Alabama. Battle of Kenesaw Mountain, Ga.
July	Battles before Atlanta, Ga. Early's Raid on Washington. The Battle of the Crater, Va.
August	Farragut's Fight at Mobile Bay, Ala.
September	Capture of Atlanta, Ga. Battle of Winchester, Va. Battle of Fisher's Hill, Va.
October	Battle of Cedar Creek, Va. Admission of Nevada.
November	Sherman's March to the Sea. Battle of Franklin, Tenn. Reëlection of President Lincoln.
December	Capture of Savannah, Ga. Battle of Nashville, Tenn.

Second Administration of Abraham Lincoln 1865

The Second Inauguration of President Lincoln
The Inaugural

"With malice toward none, with charity for all."
Lincoln.

- Blaine, i. 544.
- Draper, iii. 477-479.
- Greeley, ii. 676, 677.
- Higginson, 320, 321.
- Morse, Life of Lincoln, ii. 311-315.
- Nicolay & Hay, Life of Lincoln, x. 139-147.
- Patton, ii. 1020, 1021.
- Richardson, 583.
- Schouler, vi.
- Sheldon, 366.
- Wilson, Rise and fall of Slave Power, iii. 574-578.

Grant's Final Campaign Surrender of Lee at Appomattox

- Battles and Leaders, iv. 708-746.
- Bryant & Gay, iv. 596-598.
- Draper, iii. 560-597.
- Eggleston, 348.
- Fiske, Hist. of U.S., 382, 383.
- Greeley, Am. Conflict, ii. 726-745.
- Higginson, 316-318.
- Irving-Fiske, 575.
- Johnston, 354-356.
- Montgomery, 321.
- Morse, Life of Lincoln, ii. 337-340.
- Nicolay & Hay, Life of Lincoln, x. 148-212.
- Patton, ii. 1019-1025.
- Richardson, 579-582.
- Schouler, vi.
- Sheldon, 359-361.
- Thomas, 325, 326.
- Wilson, Epochs Am. History, 237, 238.

Campaign of 1865

Sherman's March from Savannah to Bentonville and Surrender of Johnston

- Battles and Leaders, iv. 681-695.
- Bryant & Gay, iv. 598, 599.
- Draper, iii. 539-559.
- Eggleston, 347.
- Fiske, Hist. of U.S., 382.
- Greeley, Am. Conflict, ii. 696-708.
- Higginson, 315, 316.
- Irving-Fiske, 575.
- Johnston, 353, 354.
- Montgomery, 320.
- Nicolay & Hay, Life of Lincoln, x. 229-254.
- Patton, ii. 1025.
- Richardson, 572-575.
- Schouler, vi.
- Sheldon, 356, 357.
- Thomas, 323, 324.
- Wilson, Epochs Am. History, 236.

110   *Handbook of American History*

The Assassination of the President
- Blaine, i. 546-549.
- Bryant & Gay, iv. 599.
- Draper, iii. 626-630.
- Eggleston, 354.
- Fiske, Hist. of U.S., 383, 384.
- Greeley, Am. Conflict, 746-750.
- Higginson, 322.
- Irving-Fiske, 575.
- Johnston, 358.
- Montgomery, 322.
- Morse, Life of Lincoln, ii. 342-350.
- Nicolay & Hay, Life of Lincoln, x. 286-313.
- Patton, ii. 1026.
- Richardson, 582-586.
- Schouler, vi.
- Sheldon, 362.
- Thomas, 326.
- Wilson, Epochs Am. History, 238.
- Wilson, Rise and Fall of Slave Power, iii. 579-584.

Character of Lincoln
- Blaine, i. 546-549.
- Eggleston, 354, 355.
- Fiske, Hist. of U.S., 348, 349.
- Greeley, Am. Conflict, ii. 750.
- Higginson, 322, 323.
- Morse, Life of Lincoln, ii. 354-358.
- Nicolay & Hay, Life of Lincoln, x. 341-356.
- Patton, ii. 1026.
- Richardson, 432, 433.
- Schouler, vi.
- Sheldon, 365-367.
- Thomas, 327.
- Wilson, Epochs of American History, 216, 217.
- Wilson, Rise and Fall of the Slave Power, iii. 586-588.

Period of Secession and Civil War 111

Cost of the War
in Life and
Treasure

"Altogether, while the cost of the war cannot exactly be calculated, eight billions of dollars is a moderate estimate."

{ Blaine, i. 560-562.
Draper, iii. 646, 647.
Fiske, Hist. of U.S., 393.
Greeley, ii. 759, 760.
Higginson, 318.
Johnston, 361.
Montgomery, 322.
Patton, ii. 1028.
Schouler, vi.
Thomas, 328, 329.
Wilson, Epochs Am. Hist., 252. }

The Final Reviews
and Disbanding
of the Armies

{ Draper, iii. 630-634.
Greeley, Am. Conflict, ii. 758, 759.
Higginson, 323, 324.
Johnston, 365, 366.
Montgomery, 324, 325.
Patton, ii. 1028.
Sheldon, 368, 369.
Thomas, 327, 328. }

Summary of the Events of 1865

February — Capture of Charleston, S.C.

March — { The Second Inauguration of President Lincoln.
Battle of Goldsboro, N.C. }

April — { Grant's Final Campaign and the Surrender at Appomattox.
The Assassination of the President.
Surrender of Johnston. }

June — { The Final Reviews and Disbanding of the Armies. }

Period of Reconstruction 1865–1881

Administration of Andrew Johnson 1865-1869

Establishment of Provisional Governments in the Seceded States

Restoration or reconstruction: which?

- Anderson, 328.
- Blaine, ii. 76-80.
- Johnston, Hist. Am. Politics, 197.
- Johnston, 369.
- Lalor, Cyclopædia, iii. 543, 544.
- Montgomery, 328.
- Patton, ii. 1033, 1034.
- Smith, Goldwin, 297, 298.
- Thomas, 333.
- Wilson, Epochs Am. Hist., 259.
- Wilson, Rise and Fall of Slave Power, iii. 616-618.

The XIIIth Amendment and its Adoption Dec. 18, 1865

"The necessary corollary to the Emancipation Proclamation."
"The language of the Amendment is taken almost without a change from the Ordinance of 1787."
    Thomas.
The first adoption of a constitutional Amendment for a period of sixty years.

- Anderson, 327, 328.
- Blaine, i. 504-507, 535-539.
- Eggleston, 359.
- Fiske, Hist. of U.S., 394.
- Johnston, Hist. Am. Politics, 193, 194, 195.
- Johnston, 369.
- Lalor, Cyclopædia, i. 608.
- Montgomery, 327.
- Thomas, 333.
- Wilson, Epochs Am. Hist., 259, 260.
- Wilson, Rise and Fall of Slave Power, iii. 434-454.

The Atlantic Telegraph

- Johnston, 366.
- Montgomery, 330, 331.

Period of Reconstruction

The Atlantic Telegraph
(*Continued*)
- Patton, ii. 1032.
- Richardson, 588, 589.
- Sheldon, 403.
- Thomas, 338.

The Freedmen's Bureau Bill
- Blaine, ii. 163-172.
- Fiske, Hist. of U.S., 394.
- Higginson, 324.
- Johnston, Hist. Am. Politics, 195.
- Lalor, Cyclopædia, ii. 280, 281.
- Patton, ii. 1035.
- Thomas, 334.
- Wilson, Epochs Am. Hist., 263, 264, 265.
- Wilson, Rise and Fall of Slave Power, iii. 472-504.

The Civil Rights Bill

"It conferred upon the freed negro all the civil rights enjoyed by the white man, except that of suffrage."
Blaine.

- Blaine, ii. 172-179.
- Fiske, Hist. of U.S., 394.
- Johnston, Hist. of Am. Politics, 199.
- Lalor, Cyclopædia, i. 478.
- Montgomery, 327, Note ii.
- Patton, ii. 1032, 1035.
- Thomas, 334.
- Wilson, Epochs Am. Hist., 264.
- Wilson, Rise and Fall of Slave Power, iii. 685-696.

The XIVth Amendment and its Adoption July 28, 1868

"Making permanent the provisions of the Civil Rights Bill."

- Anderson, 328.
- Blaine, ii. 245, 309, 310.
- Fiske, Hist. of U.S., 394.
- Johnston, Hist. Am. Politics, 199.
- Johnston, 371, 372.
- Lalor, Cyclopædia, i. 608.
- Montgomery, 328.
- Patton, ii. 1043.
- Thomas, 334.
- Wilson, Epochs Am. Hist., 265, 269.
- Wilson, Rise and Fall of Slave Power, iii. 647-660.

Reconstruction Acts of Congress and Appointment of Military Governors for the Seceded States

Anderson, 328.
Blaine, ii. 250-262, 292-294, 296, 297.
Higginson, 324.
Johnston, Hist. of Am. Politics, 202, 203.
Johnston, 370, 371.
Lalor, Cyclopædia, iii. 551-554, 556.
Montgomery, 328.
Patton, ii. 1043, 1044.
Sheldon, 378, 379.
Thomas, 335.
Wilson, Epochs Am. Hist., 266-268.
Wilson, Rise and Fall of Slave Power, iii. 603-630.

The "Carpet-Baggers" and the "Ku-Klux"

Blaine, ii. 304, 305, 471-475.
Fiske, Hist. of U.S., 395, 399.
Johnston, Hist. Am. Politics, 212.
Johnston, 381, 382.
Lalor, Cyclopædia, i. 354; ii. 680, 681; iii. 554.
Montgomery, 328, 329.
Patton, ii. 1054-1056.
Sheldon, 378, 404.
Thomas, 335, 336, 341, 342.
Wilson, Epochs Am. Hist., 268, 269, 274.
Wilson, Rise and Fall of Slave Power, iii. 631-646.

Purchase of Alaska 1867

Next to the Louisiana purchase, the largest acquirement of territory in our history. Price $7,200,000.

Anderson, 329.
Blaine, ii. 333-340.
Eggleston, 366.
Fiske, Hist. of U.S., 396.
Haswell, Text of Treaty, 939-942.
Higginson, 325, 326.
Johnston, 366.
Lalor, Cyclopædia, i. 98.
Montgomery, 331.
Patton, ii. 1045.
Sheldon, 403.
Thomas, 338, 339.
Wilson, Epochs Am. History, 272.

Period of Reconstruction

Impeachment of the President

See Constitution Art. I. Sect. 5; Art. III. Sect. 6.

- Anderson, 329.
- Blaine, ii. 352-384.
- Eggleston, 360.
- Fiske, Hist. of U.S., 395.
- Higginson, 325.
- Johnston, Hist. Am. Politics, 205, 206.
- Johnston, 373.
- Lalor, Cyclopædia, ii. 482-484.
- Montgomery, 329.
- Patton, ii. 1045.
- Smith, Goldwin, 299.
- Thomas, 336, 337.
- Wilson, Epochs Am. History, 270, 271.
- Wilson, Rise and Fall of Slave Power, iii. 733, 734.

Nebraska admitted, 1867.

The French in Mexico

- Blaine, i. 595-600.
- Fiske, Hist. of U.S., 396.
- Johnston, 337, 366.
- Lalor, Cyclopædia, ii. 834, 835.
- Thomas, 339, 340.
- Wilson, Epochs Am. Hist., 272.

Election of the Eighteenth President Ulysses S. Grant Reconstruction the Great Issue of the Campaign

- Anderson, 329, 330.
- Blaine, ii. 385-391, 407-408.
- Eggleston, 360.
- Fiske, Hist. of U.S., 396.
- Higginson, 326.
- Johnston, Hist. Am. Politics, 207.
- Johnston, 373.
- Lalor, Cyclopædia, ii. 59, 60.
- Montgomery, 332, Note iii.
- Patton, ii. 1046.
- Sheldon, 404.
- Stanwood, Presidential Elections, 256-275.
- Thomas, 337.
- Wilson, Epochs Am. History, 271, 272.
- Wilson, Rise and Fall of Slave Power, iii. 734, 735.

First Administration of U. S. Grant 1869-1873

Completion of the Central Pacific Railway The First Trans-Continental Line
- Johnston, 378.
- Lalor, Cyclopædia, ii.572; iii. 513, 514.
- Montgomery, 332-334.
- Patton, ii. 1047.
- Sheldon, 397, 398.
- Thomas, 341.

XVth Amendment to the Constitution Mar. 30, 1870

"It gave the negro the right to vote."
- Blaine, ii. 465, 466.
- Eggleston, 360.
- Fiske, Hist. of U.S., 399.
- Higginson, 326.
- Johnston, Hist. of Am. Politics, 207, 208.
- Johnston, 380.
- Lalor, Cyclopædia, i. 608.
- Montgomery, 330.
- Patton, ii. 1047, 1048.
- Thomas, 342, 343.
- Wilson, Epochs Am. History, 269, 270.

The Treaty of Washington The Alabama Claims and the Geneva Award
- Anderson, 330-332.
- Blaine, ii. 476-485, 493-502.
- Eggleston, 352.
- Fiske, Hist. of U.S., 398.
- Haswell, Treaties and Conventions, 478-499.
- Higginson, 326, 327.
- Johnston, Hist. Am. Politics, 214.
- Johnston, 375, 376.
- Lalor, Cyclopædia, ii. 331-333.
- Montgomery, 339.
- Patton, ii. 1049-1053.
- Sheldon, 379, 380.
- Thomas, 345-347.
- Wilson, Epochs Am. History, 278, 279.

Two Great Fires
- Johnston, 378, 379.
- Montgomery, 336.
- Patton, ii. 1057, 1058.
- Thomas, 347, 348.

Period of Reconstruction

The Credit Mobilier Bribery of Members of Congress by the Union Pacific Railroad Company
- Johnston, Hist. Am. Politics, 219, 220.
- Johnston, 382, 383.
- Lalor, Cyclopædia, i. 709; iii. 513.
- Montgomery, 333.
- Sheldon, 404.
- Thomas, 351, 352.
- Wilson, Epochs Am. History, 279, 280.

Re-election of President Grant
- Anderson, 332.
- Blaine, ii. 516-536.
- Eggleston, 361.
- Fiske, Hist. of U.S., 400.
- Johnston, Hist. Am. Politics, 217-221.
- Johnston, 383.
- Lalor, Cyclopædia, ii. 60.
- Patton, ii. 1064.
- Sheldon, 404.
- Stanwood, Presidential Elections, 276-301.
- Thomas, 348, 349.
- Wilson, Epochs Am. History, 281, 282.

Second Administration of U. S. Grant 1873-1877

Financial Panic of 1873
"A necessary consequence of the speculation and over-production incited by the inflated currency of the war period."
- Blaine, ii. 561.
- Fiske, Hist. of U.S., 400, 401.
- Johnston, 377.
- Lalor, Cyclopædia, iii. 1000.
- Montgomery, 377.
- Patton, ii. 1059.
- Thomas, 350.

The Resumption Act
- Blaine, ii. 563-565.
- Fiske, Hist. of U.S., 403.
- Higginson, 338, 339.
- Johnston, Hist. Am. Politics, 227.
- Johnston, 390, 391.
- Lalor, Cyclopædia, ii. 195; iii. 1000.
- Montgomery, 342, 343.

The Resumption
Act
(*Continued*)
{ Patton, ii. 1060.
Thomas, 354.
Wilson, Epochs Am. History, 280.

Colorado admitted, 1876.   The "Centennial State."

The Centennial
Exposition
Philadelphia
1876

"They are milestones of progress."
Blanqui.

{ Anderson, 332, 333.
Fiske, Hist. of U.S., 401.
Higginson, 330, 331.
Johnston, Hist. Am. Politics, 230, 231.
Johnston, 379, 380.
Lalor, Cyclopædia, ii. 140.
Montgomery, 337, 338.
Patton, ii. 1063, 1064.
Sheldon, 405.
Thomas, 354, 355.
Wilson, Epochs Am. History, 286, 287.

Two Indian Wars
The Modoc
and the Sioux

{ Eggleston, 367-370.
Fiske, Hist. of U.S., 401.
Johnston, 379.
Montgomery, 339.
Patton, ii. 1061, 1062.
Sheldon, 404, 405.
Thomas, 349, 350, 355.

Election of the
Nineteenth
President
Rutherford
B. Hayes

{ Anderson, 336.
Blaine, ii. 567-582.
Eggleston, 361.
Fiske, Hist. of U.S., 401-403.
Higginson, 331-333.
Johnston, Hist. Am. Politics, 231-234.
Johnston, 384.
Lalor, Cyclopædia, ii. 60.
Montgomery, 340, Note.
Patton, ii. 1069, 1070.
Sheldon, 405.
Stanwood, Presidential Elections, 306-331.
Thomas, 356-358.
Wilson, Epochs Am. History, 283-285.

Period of Reconstruction

The Disputed Election and the Electoral Commission
- Anderson, 337.
- Blaine, ii. 582-589.
- Eggleston, 361, 362.
- Fiske, Hist. of U.S., 402, 403.
- Higginson, 333, 334.
- Johnston, Hist. Am. Politics, 234-237.
- Johnston, 385, 386.
- Lalor, Cyclopædia, i. 786, 808; ii. 50-53.
- Montgomery, 340, Note.
- Patton, ii. 1070.
- Sheldon, 405.
- Stanwood, Presidential Elections, 332-344.
- Thomas, 358-359.
- Wilson, Epochs Am. History, 285, 286.

Administration of Rutherford B. Hayes 1877-1881

Withdrawal of Troops from the Southern States
- Anderson, 337.
- Blaine, ii. 595, 596.
- Fiske, Hist. of U.S., 403.
- Higginson, 335.
- Johnston, Hist. Am. Politics, 238.
- Johnston, 387.
- Lalor, Cyclopædia, iii. 1000.
- Montgomery, 340.
- Patton, ii. 1073.
- Thomas, 361.
- Wilson, Epochs Am. History, 286.

The Bland Silver Bill remonetizes Silver
- Blaine, ii. 602-610.
- Johnston, Hist. Am. Politics, 239, 240.
- Johnston, 390.
- Lalor, Cyclopædia, iii. 602, 603.
- Montgomery, 342, Note iii.
- Patton, ii. 1073.
- Thomas, 362.
- Wilson, Epochs Am. History, 291, 292.

The Mississippi Jetties
- Johnston, 389.
- Montgomery, 341, 342.
- Thomas, 364.

The Fisheries Commission and the Halifax Award

Arranged for by the Treaty of 1871 with Great Britain.
- Blaine, ii. 631-637.
- Haswell, Treaties and Conventions, 487. 488.
- Johnston, 376.
- Lalor, Cyclopædia, iii. 943.
- Montgomery, 339, Note ii.
- Patton, ii. 1074.
- Thomas, 347.
- Wilson, Epochs Am. History, 278.

Specie Payments resumed Jan. 1, 1879 after nearly Eighteen Years of Paper Currency
- Anderson, 338.
- Blaine, ii. 610, 611.
- Fiske, Hist. of U.S., 403.
- Higginson, 338, 339.
- Johnston, Hist. Am. Politics, 241.
- Johnston, 390, 391.
- Lalor, Cyclopædia, iii. 602, 1000.
- Montgomery, 342, 343.
- Patton, ii. 1074.
- Thomas, 364, 365.
- Wilson, Epochs Am. History, 280, 281.

Election of the Twentieth President James A. Garfield Chester A. Arthur Vice-President
- Anderson, 339.
- Blaine, ii. 657-670.
- Eggleston, 362.
- Fiske, Hist. of U.S. 404.
- Higginson. 340, 341.
- Johnston, History of Am. Politics, 244-246.
- Johnston, 392.
- Lalor, Cyclopædia, ii. 60, 326, 327.
- Montgomery, 343.
- Patton, ii. 1076, 1082.
- Stanwood, Presidential Elections, 354-374.
- Thomas, 365.
- Wilson, Epochs Am. History, 288.

Summary of the Period of Reconstruction 1865-1881

1865
- Succession of Vice-President Andrew Johnson.
- Establishment of Provisional Governments in the Seceded States.
- Adoption of the XIIIth Amendment to the Constitution.

1866
- The Atlantic Telegraph Cable.
- The Freedmen's Bureau Bill.
- The Civil Rights Bill.

1867
- Purchase of Alaska.
- The Reconstruction Acts of Congress.
- The French in Mexico.
- Impeachment of President Johnson.
- Nebraska Admitted.

1868
- The Carpet-Baggers.
- Adoption of the XIVth Amendment to the Constitution.
- Election of Ulysses S. Grant.

1869
- Inauguration of President Grant.
- Completion of the Central Pacific Railway.

1870
- Adoption of the XVth Amendment to the Constitution.

1871
- The Treaty of Washington.
- The Great Fire at Chicago.
- The Credit Mobilier.

1872
- Reëlection of President Grant.
- The Modoc Indian War.
- The Great Fire at Boston.

1873
- Financial Panic.

1875
- The Resumption Act.

1876
- Colorado Admitted.
- The Centennial Exposition at Philadelphia.
- The Sioux Indian War.
- The Election of Rutherford B. Hayes.

1877
- The Disputed Election and Electoral Commission.
- Withdrawal of Troops from the South.

1878
- The Bland Silver Bill.
- The Mississippi Jetties.
- The Halifax Award.

1879
- Specie Payments resumed.

1880
- Election of James A. Garfield and Chester A. Arthur.

Period of Recent Growth 1881-1889

The Assassination of President Garfield and the Succession of President Arthur

"The President's assassination served at least one useful purpose: it threw a vivid light upon the evils of the American system of appointments to, and removals from, office." *Johnston.*

- Anderson, 340.
- Blaine, ii. 676.
- Eggleston, 362.
- Fiske, Hist. of U.S., 406.
- Higginson, 341, 342.
- Johnston, Hist. Am. Politics, 247.
- Johnston, 394.
- Lalor, Cyclopædia, ii. 326, 327.
- Montgomery, 343.
- Patton, ii. 1082-1092.
- Stanwood, Presidential Elections, 375.
- Thomas, 366.
- Wilson, Epochs Am. History, 289.

Administration of Chester A. Arthur 1881-1885

The Yorktown Centennial
- Johnston, 395.
- Patton, ii. 1096.
- Thomas, 370, 371.

The Edmunds Anti-Polygamy Bill
- Johnston, 395.
- Lalor, Cyclopædia, iii. 1044.
- Sheldon, 405.
- Thomas, 367.
- Wilson, Epochs Am. History, 297, 298.

Civil Service under President Arthur
- Fiske, Hist. of U.S., 406.
- Johnston, Hist. Am. Politics, 247.
- Johnston, 394, 395.
- Lalor, Cyclopædia, iii. 485.
- Montgomery, 344.

124   *Handbook of American History*

Civil Service under President Arthur
(*Continued*)
- Patton, ii. 1097, 1104, 1105.
- Stanwood, Presidential Elections, 376.
- Thomas, 367, 368.
- Wilson, Epochs American History, 293.

The Tariff Commission, and the Revision of 1883
"The first general revision since the war." *Taussig.*
- Johnston, 396.
- Lalor, Cyclopædia, iii. 866, 867.
- Patton, ii. 1102-1104.
- Taussig, History of the Tariff, 230-258.
- Thomas, 368, 369.
- Wilson, Epochs Am. History, 290, 291.

Election of the Twenty-Second President Grover Cleveland
Protection *vs.* Free Trade the one great issue of the Campaign.
- Anderson, 341.
- Eggleston, 363.
- Fiske, Hist. of U.S., 406.
- Higginson, 343.
- Johnston, 396, 397.
- Montgomery, 349.
- Patton, ii. 1110.
- Stanwood, Presidential Elections, 384-411.
- Thomas, 373, 374.
- Wilson, Epochs Am. History. 289.

First Administration of Grover Cleveland 1885-1889

Act for the Presidential Succession
- Johnston, 399.
- Montgomery, 354, Note i.
- Patton, ii. 1125.
- Stanwood, Presidential Elections, 412-414.
- Thomas, 375, 376.
- Wilson, Epochs Am. History, 296, 297.

The Inter-State Commerce Act
- Johnston, 399.
- Montgomery, 354.
- Patton, ii. 1126, 1127.
- Thomas, 376.
- Wilson, Epochs Am. History, 294-296.

The Act for the Counting of Electoral Votes

The Principle embodied in this act was the rule acted upon by the Electoral Commission that seated President Hayes.

- Johnston, 399.
- Montgomery, 354.
- Patton, ii. 1126.
- Stanwood, Presidential Elections, 415-419.
- Thomas, 376.
- Wilson, Epochs Am. History, 296.

The Chinese Exclusion Act

- Johnston, 391, 398.
- Montgomery, 354.
- Thomas, 376, 377.
- Wilson, Epochs Am. History, 297.

Labor Troubles and Anarchists

- Johnston, 397, 398.
- Montgomery, 351, 352.
- Thomas, 377-379.

Election of the Twenty-Third President Benj. Harrison Nov. 1888

- Fiske, Hist. of U.S., 407.
- Johnston, 400.
- Montgomery, 355, Note iii.
- Patton, ii. 1127, 1128.
- Stanwood, Presidential Elections, 421-439.
- Thomas, 381, 382.

Close of the First Century of our Constitutional History 1889

- Johnston, 400, 402, 403.
- Montgomery, 359.
- Patton, ii. 1139, 1140.
- Wilson, Epochs Am. History, 298, 299.

Summary of Period of Recent Growth 1881-1889

1880	Inauguration of President Garfield.
1881	{ Assassination of President Garfield and the Succession of President Arthur. The Yorktown Centennial.
1882	The Edmunds Anti-Polygamy Bill.
1883	{ Civil Service Act. The Tariff Commission and Revision of 1883.
1884	Election of Grover Cleveland.
1885	Inauguration of President Cleveland.
1886	Act for the Presidential Succession.
1887	{ Inter-State Commerce Act. Act for the Counting of Electoral Votes.
1888	{ The Chinese Exclusion Act. Labor Troubles and Anarchists. Election of Benjamin Harrison.
1889	{ Close of the First Century of Constitutional History.

"THE EQUILIBRIUM OF PARTIES TEMPERS POLITICAL ACTION, AND THE PRESENCE OF NEW PROBLEMS QUICKENS SOBER THOUGHT, AND DISPOSES THE NATION TO CAREFUL DEBATE OF ITS FUTURE."

Woodrow Wilson.

PARTY RECORDS IN AMERICAN HISTORY

"To the close of the Administration of Benjamin Harrison, a period of 104 years of our National Life under the Constitution, political power has been placed for exactly equal periods, 52 years, with the Democratic and Republican Parties, or their predecessors in pedigree."

A GENERAL STATEMENT OF PARTY RECORDS IN AMERICAN CONSTITUTIONAL HISTORY.

Names.	Duration.	Favored or Opposed Large National Powers.	Favored or Opposed Easy Terms of Suffrage and Naturalization.	Favored or Opposed Government Patronage of Internal Improvements.	Favored or Opposed Slavery and the Acquirement of Slave Territory.	Favored or Opposed a Protective Tariff.	Special or Distinctive Principle of Party Platforms.
Anti-Federalist.	1789-1796.	Opposed.	Favored.	Opposed.	Not on Record.	Not on Record.	Strict Construction of the Powers of the Constitution, and Support of State Governments.
Democratic-Republican.	1796-1812.	Opposed.	Favored.	Opposed.	Favored.	Not on Record.	Lenience toward State Authority.
Democratic.	1812 to the Present.	Opposes.	Favors.	Opposes.	Favored.	Opposes.	Lenient toward Slavery. Opposed to Large National Powers. Favors Free Trade or Revenue Tariff.
Federalist.	1788-1820.	Favored.	Opposed.	Favored.	Opposed.	Favored.	Liberal Construction of the Powers of the Constitution, and Liberal Support of the National Government.
Free-Soil.	1845-1856.	Favored.	Indifferent.	Favored.	Opposed.	Favored.	The Non-extension of Slavery to Territories.
Know-Nothing, or American.	1852-1856.	Favored.	Opposed.	Favored.	Divided into Northern and South'n Wings.	Favored.	Nativism, or Opposition to the Alien.
National Prohibition.	1869 to the Present.	Favors.	Opposes.	Opposes.	Not on Record.	Opposes.	Prohibition of the Manufacture and Sale of Intoxicants.
Republican.	1855 to the Present.	Favors.	Opposes.	Favors.	Opposed.	Favors.	Opposition to the further Extension of Slavery. The Integrity of the Union. Protection to American Industries.
Whig.	1836-1852.	Favored.	Opposed.	Favored.	Divided into Northern and Southern Wings.	Favored.	Support of the "American System" of Protection, and Internal Improvements.

(129)

INDEX

A

	PAGE
Act for Counting the Electoral Vote	125
Adams, John, Election of	12
Adams, John, Death of	43
Adams, John Quincy, Election of	42
Addresses, Newburgh	2
Admission of New States	8
Aggressions on Neutral Trade	22
Alabama Admitted	36
Alabama and Kearsarge, Duel of	106
Alabama Claims	116
Alaska, Purchase of	114
Algerine War	33
Alien and Sedition Acts	14
Amendment, The XIIth	20
Amendment, The XIIIth, to the Constitution	113
Amendment, The XIVth, to the Constitution	113
Amendment, The XVth, to the Constitution	116
American Party	74
American System	39
Anarchists	125
Antietam, Battle of	95
Anti-Federalist Party	8
Anti-Polygamy Bill	123
Anti-Slavery Movement	51
Anti-Slavery Revolt	67
Anti-Slavery Society	51
Appomattox, Surrender at	109
Arkansas Admitted	53
Arthur, Chester A., his Succession	123
Articles of Confederation	1
Ashburton Treaty	59
Assassination of President Lincoln	110
Assassination of President Garfield	123
Assumption of State Debts	9

B

Baltimore, Attack on	30
Bank Deposits, Removal of	50
Bank, Incorporation of the First	9
Banking, National	101
Barbary States, Subjection of	33
Barbary Wars	18
Battle, First, of the Ironclads	92
Berlin Decrees	22
Black Hawk War	48
Bland Silver Bill	119
Boundary, The Northwest	38
British Orders in Council	22
Brown, John, his Raid	82
Buchanan, James, Election of	77
Buffalo Convention	67
Bull Run, First Battle of	90
Bull Run, Second Battle of	95
Burns, Anthony, Case of	73
Burnside at Fredericksburg	96
Burr, Duel of, with Hamilton	20

C

Cabinet, The First	7
California Admitted	69
Call to Arms, The	88
Campaigns of war of 1812	28–32
Campaign of 1862 in the West	93
Capitol, Establishment of, at Washington	15
Caroline Affair	55
Carpet-Baggers	114
Cedar Creek, Battle of	104
Cedar Mountain, Battle of	95
Centennial Exposition of 1876	118
Century, Close of the First	125
Chancellorsville, Battle of	98
Charleston Convention	83
Chattanooga, Battle of	100
Chesapeake Outrage	27
Chesapeake, Loss of the	29
Chickamauga, Battle of	100
Chinese Exclusion Act	125
Chippewa, Battle of	30
Civil Rights Bill	113
Civil Service under President Arthur	123
Clay, Death and Character of	71

Index

	PAGE
Cleveland, Election of	124
Colorado Admitted	118
Commanders, The new	102
Compromise of 1850	69
Compromise Tariff	50
Compromises in Constitution	5
Confederation, Articles of	1
Confederation, Defects of	1
Confederate Cruisers	106
Confederate Government, Establishment of	87
Conspiracy of Aaron Burr	21
Constitution, Compromises in	5
Constitution, Ratification of	5
Constitution, Sources of	4
Convention, Constitutional	3
Convention, The Hartford	31
Correspondence of Webster and Hülseman	71
Cotton Gin	10
Credit Mobilier	117
Creek Indians	41
Crittenden Compromise	85
Cuban Filibusters	71
Cumberland Road	39

D

Deaths of Adams and Jefferson	43
Decatur's Exploit	18
Democratic Party, Split in	83
Disorders in the States	2
Dissatisfaction in New England	31
Division of Parties	8
Dorr's Rebellion	59
Draft and Draft Riots	101
Dred Scott Decision	80
Duel of Burr and Hamilton	20
Duels, Four Great Ship	28

E

Edmunds' Anti-Polygamy Bill	123
Election of Washington	7
Election of John Adams	12
Election of Thomas Jefferson	18
Election of James Madison	25
Election of James Monroe	34
Election of John Quincy Adams	42
Election of Andrew Jackson	44
Election of Martin Van Buren	53
Election of Wm. Henry Harrison	56
Election of John Tyler	56
Election of James K. Polk	61
Election of Zachary Taylor	68
Election of Millard Fillmore	68
Election of Franklin Pierce	72
Election of James Buchanan	77
Election of Abraham Lincoln	84

	PAGE
Election of Andrew Johnson	107
Election of Ulysses S. Grant	115
Election of Rutherford B. Hayes	118
Election of James A. Garfield	120
Election of Chester A. Arthur	120
Election of Grover Cleveland	124
Election of Benjamin Harrison	125
Election, The Disputed	119
Electoral Commission	119
Emancipation	98
Embargo	23
England's Aggressions on Neutral Trade	22
Era of Good Feeling	39
Erie Canal	40
Essex, The Cruise of the	30
Establishment of the New Government	7
Ether first used	60
Excise, The First	9

F

Farragut's Capture of New Orleans	93
Farragut's Battle of Mobile Bay	106
Federalist, The	5
Federalist Party	8
Federalist Party, Downfall of	16
Filibuster Expedition to Cuba	71
Fillmore, Millard, Election of	71
Final Reviews and Disbanding of the Armies of 1865	111
Financial Measures of Hamilton	9
Fires, Two Great	116
Fisheries Commission	120
Fisher's Hill, Battle of	104
Florida, Purchase of	38
Florida Admitted	60
Fort Donelson, Capture of	93
Fort Henry, Capture of	93
France, Troubles with	13
Franklin, Battle of	105
Fredericksburg, Battle of	96
Freedmen's Bureau Bill	113
Free-Soil Party, Formation of	67
Fremont's Campaign in California	64
French Revolution, Influence on American Politics	11
French Spoliation Claims	53
French, The, in Mexico	115
Friction Matches	55
Fugitive Slave Law	70
Fulton, Robert, his Steamboat	22
Funding Bill	9

G

Gadsden Purchase	74
Garfield, Election of	120

Index

	PAGE
Garfield, Assassination of	123
Garrison, Wm. Lloyd	51
Genet, Citizen	10
Geneva Award	116
Georgia and the Creek Indians	42
Gettysburg, Battle of	99
Ghent, Treaty of	32
Gold, Discovery of	67
Grant, Appointed Lieut.-Gen.	102
Grant, his Campaign to the James,	103
Grant, his Final Campaign	109
Grant, Election of	115
Grant, Reëlection of	117
Guadalupe Hidalgo, Treaty of	66

H

Halifax Award	120
Hamilton, Financial Measures of	9
Hamilton, Duel of, with Burr	20
Harrison, Benjamin, Election of	125
Harrison, Wm. Henry, Election of,	56
Hartford Convention	31
Hayes, Rutherford B., Election of,	118
Hood's Sortie to Tennessee	105
Hooker at Chancellorsville	98
Hull's Surrender	28

I

Illinois Admitted	36
Impeachment of President Johnson,	115
Independence of Texas	52
Independent Treasury	54
India Rubber	55
Indiana Admitted	34
Indian Wars, The Blackhawk and Osceola	48
Indian Wars, The Modoc and the Sioux	118
Internal Improvements	39
Inter-State Commerce Act	124
Iowa Admitted	63
Ironclads, First Battle of	92

J

Jackson, Andrew, Victory at New Orleans	32
Jackson, Andrew, Election of	44
Jay, Treaty of	11
Jefferson, Thomas, Election and Inauguration of	18
Jefferson, Thomas, Retirement of	24
Jefferson, Thomas, Death of	43
Jefferson, Thomas, Character of	24
Jetties, The Mississippi	120
Johnson, Andrew, Election of	107

	PAGE
Johnson, Andrew, Impeachment of,	115
Johnston, Surrender of	109

K

Kansas-Nebraska Bill	73
Kansas, The Struggle for	75
Kansas, The Topeka and Lecompton Constitutions	80
Kansas Admitted	85
Kearney's Campaign in New Mexico	64
Kentucky Admitted	8
Kitchen Cabinet, The	47
Know-Nothing or American Party,	74
Ku-Klux Klans	114

L

Labor Troubles	125
Lafayette, Visit of	41
Lee's Campaign against Pope	95
Lee's Invasion of Maryland	95
Lee's Second Invasion of Maryland,	99
Lee's Surrender at Appomattox	109
Legal-Tender Act	101
Leopard and Chesapeake, Affair of,	23
Lewis and Clarke Expedition	20
Lincoln-Douglas Debates	82
Lincoln, Election of	84
Lincoln, President	87
Lincoln, Reëlection of	107
Lincoln, Second Inauguration of	108
Lincoln, Character of	110
Lincoln, Assassination of	110
Lines of Division between Slave and Free Territory	36
Literature, American	52
Locomotive, Introduction of	51
Log-rolling, First Case of	15
Louisiana, Purchase of	19
Louisiana, Admitted	27
Lundy's Lane, Battle of	30

M

MacDonough's Victory	31
Madison, Election of	25
Maine Admitted	37
March, Sherman's, from Atlanta to the Sea	105
Mexican War in General	63
Michigan Admitted	53
Milan Decree	22
Minnesota Admitted	82
Mississippi Admitted	34
Mississippi Jetties	120
Mississippi, Reopening of the	100

	PAGE
Missouri Compromise	36
Missouri Admitted	38
Missouri Compromise, Repeal of,	73
Mobile Bay, Battle of	106
Monitor and Merrimac	92
Monroe, Election of	34
Monroe Doctrine	41
Mormons, The	60
Mormons, Rebellion of, 1857	82
Morrill Tariff of 1861	86
Murfreesboro, Battle of	93

N

Nashville, Battle of	105
National Bank, Jackson's Hostility to	49
National Banking System	101
Nebraska Admitted	115
Nevada Admitted	104
Newburgh Addresses	2
New Orleans, Battle of	32
New Orleans, Capture of by Farragut	93
Northwest Boundary, Temporary Settlement of	38
Northwest Territory	3
Nullification and Calhoun	49

O

Office, Removals from	48
Ohio Admitted	19
Omnibus Bill	69
Ordinance of 1787	3
Oregon Discovery	20
Oregon Boundary Dispute	61
Oregon Admitted	83
Osceola	48
Ostend Manifesto	75

P

Pacific Railroad, The Central	116
Panama Congress, Attempt at a	42
Panic of 1837	51
Panic of 1857	81
Panic of 1873	117
Parties, Division of	8
Peninsula Campaign	94
Perry's Japan Expedition	71
Perryville, Battle of	93
Perry's Victory	30
Personal Liberty and Homestead Laws	81
Petersburg, Nine Months' Siege of,	103
Petition, Right of	55
Petroleum Discovered	84
Pierce, Franklin, Administration of,	73

	PAGE
Policy of Hesitation	85
Polk, James K., Election of	61
President, Change in the Mode of Electing	19
President Lincoln	87
Presidential Nominations	43
Presidential Succession, Act for	124
Provisional Governments, Establishment of	112

Q

Queenstown, Battle of	28

R

Railway System, Introduction of	51
Ratification of Constitution	5
Reams Station, Battle of	104
Rebellion, Shays'	2
Reconstruction Acts of Congress	114
Removal of the Bank Deposits	50
Republican Party, Rise of	76
Resumption of Specie Payments, 117,	120
Riots, Slavery	55

S

Savannah, Capture of	105
Scott's Campaign in Central Mexico	65
Secession of the Seven Cotton States	84
Secession of Four Other States	89
Second Bull Run, Battle of	95
Sedition Acts	14
Seminole War	37
Sewing Machine Patented	62
Shays' Rebellion	2
Sheridan's Campaign against Early	104
Sherman, Commands Army of the West	102
Sherman's Campaign from Chattanooga to Atlanta	104
Sherman's March from Atlanta to the Sea	105
Sherman's March from Savannah to Bentonville	106
Shiloh, Battle of	93
Slave Trade Forbidden	24
Slavery Agitation, Beginnings of	36
Slavery Riots	55
Specie Payments Resumed	120
Squatter Sovereignty	73
States, Admission of	8
Sub-Treasury, The	54
Summary of Critical Period	6
Summary of Period of Federalist Supremacy	16

Index

	PAGE
Summary of the Period of Republican supremacy	25
Summary of the Period of Foreign War	35
Summary of the Period of National Growth	45
Summary of the Period of Critical Change	57
Summary of the Period of Slavery Agitation	77
Summary of the Period of Secession and Civil War	85
Summary of Events of 1861	91
Summary of Events of 1862	97
Summary of Events of 1863	102
Summary of Events of 1864	107
Summary of Events of 1865	111
Summary of the Period of Reconstruction	121
Summary of the Period of Recent Growth	126
Sumner, Charles, Assault on	76
Sumter, Fall of	88
Surrender of Hull	28
Surrender of Lee	109
Surrender of Johnston	109

T

Tariff, First Protective	33
Tariff of 1824	40
Tariff of Abominations	44
Tariff Compromise of 1833	50
Tariff of 1842	58
Tariff of 1846	66
Tariff of 1857	81
Tariff of 1861	86
Tariff Revision of 1883	124
Tariff Commission	124
Taylor's Campaign in Northern Mexico	63
Taylor, Election of	68
Tecumseh	27
Tecumseh, Death of	29
Telegraph, The First Electric	60
Telegraph, The Atlantic	112
Tennessee Admitted	8
Tennessee Campaign of 1863	100
Texas, Independence of	52
Texas Annexation	58
Texas Boundary Dispute	62
Texas Admitted	62
Thames, Battle of the	29

	PAGE
Tippecanoe, Battle of	27
Topeka and Lecompton Constitutions	80
Treaty of Jay	11
Treaty of Ghent	32
Treaty of Guadalupe Hidalgo	66
Treaty of Washington	59, 120
Trent, Affair of the	91
Troops, Withdrawal of, from Southern States	119
Tyler, Election of	56

U

Uncle Tom's Cabin	72

V

Vaccination introduced	15
Van Buren, Election of	53
Vermont Admitted	8
Vicksburg, Siege and Capture of	100
Virginia and Kentucky Resolutions	14

W

War of 1812, Causes of	27
War of the Rebellion, Cost of	111
War Measures of Special Session of Congress, 1861	90
Washington, Administrations of	7–12
Washington, Inauguration of	7
Washington, Farewell Address of	12
Washington, Death of	15
Washington City, Attack on	30
Webster-Hayne Debate	47
Webster, Correspondence of, with Hülsemann	71
Webster-Ashburton Treaty	59
Webster's Seventh of March Speech	69
Webster, Death of	72
West Virginia Admitted	97
Whig Party, Death of	72
Whiskey Insurrection	9
Wilmot Proviso	65
Winchester, Battle of	104
Wisconsin Admitted	67

Y

Yorktown Centennial	123

www.ingramcontent.com/pod-product-compliance
Lightning Source LLC
Chambersburg PA
CBHW021729220426
43662CB00008B/771